Br

TOM BRADY

A CELEBRATION OF GREATNESS ON THE GRIDIRON

TOM BRADY

A CELEBRATION OF GREATNESS ON THE GRIDIRON

DAVID FISCHER

LYONS PRESS

Guilford, Connecticut

An imprint of Globe Pequot, trade division of The Rowman & Littlefield Publishing Group, Inc.
4501 Forbes Blvd., Ste. 200
Lanham, MD 20706
www.LyonsPress.com

Distributed by NATIONAL BOOK NETWORK

British Library Cataloguing in Publication Information available

Library of Congress Control Number: 2021932931

ISBN 978-1-4930-5222-6 (cloth: alk. paper)
ISBN 978-1-4930-5913-3 (electronic)

♾™ The paper used in this publication meets the minimum requirements of American National Standard for Information Sciences—Permanence of Paper for Printed Library Materials, ANSI/NISO Z39.48-1992.

For my sister, Betsy.
I can always count on you.

CONTENTS

PREFACE

TOM BRADY HAS BEEN A BIG PART OF MY SON'S LIFE FOR nearly two decades. That may sound odd, given that Jack resides in the New York area—the heart of Giants Country. But in February 2008, ten-year-old Jack was rooting hard against Big Blue when the Patriots played them in Super Bowl XLII. And I couldn't blame him.

You see, I work as a freelance journalist. In the spring of 2002, while I was on assignment for *Sports Illustrated Kids* magazine, my son and I were playing with building blocks when the telephone rang. Jack, then five years old, and honing his already impressive telephone reaction skills, dashed to answer the bell.

"Hello, may I help you?" he said. (He once was adorable.)

Now, as I stood nearby, waiting to be handed the phone, I listened to a one-sided conversation as my son began answering the caller's questions.

"Jack," he said.

"Baseball."

"Second base."

"Yankees."

"Derek Jeter."

"Kindergarten."

"Storytime is my favorite."

"Okay, my dad's right here. Bye."

Jack handed me the phone.

"Hello," I said, expecting the caller to identify himself as a family friend, and a child-tolerant one at that.

"Mr. Fischer, this is Tom Brady. I understand you'd like to interview me."

You can imagine my shock and awe to learn the identity of the mysterious caller. For here was Brady, a twenty-four-year-old California kid fresh off winning his first Super Bowl championship as the game's most valuable player, engaging my child in idle chitchat! And not just any child, mind you, but a sportswriter's child. This Brady guy gets it, I thought; he is something special.

As the years passed, and Brady's legend grew, Jack began to understand how lucky he had been to answer the telephone on that faraway day. He still proudly tells envious friends about his conversation with Brady, and he has truly reveled in Brady's on-field successes.

Of course, he owned a No. 12 Patriots jersey, and he was allowed to stay up past his bedtime whenever New England appeared on the NFL's Sunday- or Monday-night telecasts. Jack's bedroom walls were festooned with posters of record-setting athletes, but the most prominent spaces were reserved for Brady's image. Nineteen years later, Jack's favorite pro football player is still Brady—and I couldn't be happier with the role model he has chosen.

As the 2007 NFL season played out, and the Patriots reeled off victory after victory into early December, Jack and I began to discuss the possible scenarios of the Patriots–Giants regular-season game scheduled for Week 17. Rooting for Brady's Patriots to beat the Giants—which meant rooting against his friends—was not difficult for Jack to explain to his pals. The Giants, after all, were already playoff-bound, while the Patriots were streaking to the most perfectly perfect season in league history. According to Jack, his decision to throw his support to Brady was a no-brainer, no need for review. He was rooting for history.

The Patriots did achieve a perfect regular-season record, and then won two more postseason games to punch a ticket to the Super Bowl. There, they'd face the Giants once again. I was curious as to what Jack's reaction would be to this fanatical conundrum. Would he outwardly root for Brady, or keep his preference to himself?

The resounding answer was proclaimed on the first morning he returned to school after the league championship games. Jack came into the kitchen for his pancake breakfast wearing his Patriots No. 12 home jersey, with an additional message of his own design. With the use of construction paper, a black marker, and what must've been 10 yards of masking tape, Jack had affixed a handwritten sign to the back of his Brady jersey that read: "GIANTS NEED LUCK."

The Pats could've used a little luck. By the end of Super Bowl XLII, one young fan in our home wearing his Patriots jersey clearly was upset about the outcome. Not just because the Patriots lost, but because Brady did. My son's hero, at least for this one game, had fallen—mightily. This was a teachable moment for a ten-year-old: about the ideals of sportsmanship, the joys of competition, giving your all as a valued member of a team, being proud of one's accomplishments without regard to final score, and, finally, the importance of working hard to improve for next time.

But I struggled to get the words out. The room was oddly silent.

Eventually, Jack's face broke into a wide grin. He'd had an epiphany.

"I still love Tom Brady," he told me.

Yes, I thought. I am a great dad. I'd raised a great kid.

Jack is now twenty-three, and still rooting hard for Tom Brady. So much has changed, and yet, nothing has changed.

I wonder how much Tom Brady has changed. After all these years, he's still under center, barking signals, and playing quarterback for the dominant team in the NFL. More amazing, whether in New England or now in Tampa, he continues to beat back every challenger, overcome every challenge, every season, year after year, time after time.

He makes a heck of a role model.

CHAPTER 1
CALIFORNIA KID

TOM BRADY WAS BORN THOMAS EDWARD PATRICK BRADY JR. on August 3, 1977, in San Mateo, California, an affluent Silicon Valley suburb of about 100,000 people located some 25 miles south of San Francisco. He was the youngest of four children born to Galynn and Thomas Brady. His father, known as Tom Sr., worked in insurance and as an estate planner, with offices in the Bay Area, New York, and Boston, while his mother stayed at home to care for the family. When Tommy—the name his family still calls him—came into this world, his parents already had three daughters. Maureen was born in 1973. The second child, Julie, arrived the following year, and Nancy came along in 1976.

Brady was raised on Portola Drive in the same house where his parents still live. Homes on the tree-lined street were modest in size and closely spaced. The neighborhood was teeming with kids, which made it easy for a genial kid like Tommy to make friends. The nearby playgrounds served as gathering spots where he and his friends climbed on jungle gyms and rode seesaws. The neighborhood kids competed with ruthless aggression in favorite games like kickball, basketball, baseball, soccer, and touch football.

Brady grew up in a family that was athletically talented and enthusiastic about competition. His father, Tom Sr., was an excellent golfer, and also once regularly played in a men's basketball league. His mother, Galynn, was an avid tennis player who also developed a real talent for golf, and she played on competitive soccer teams into her forties. Maureen, Julie, and Nancy played soccer and softball,

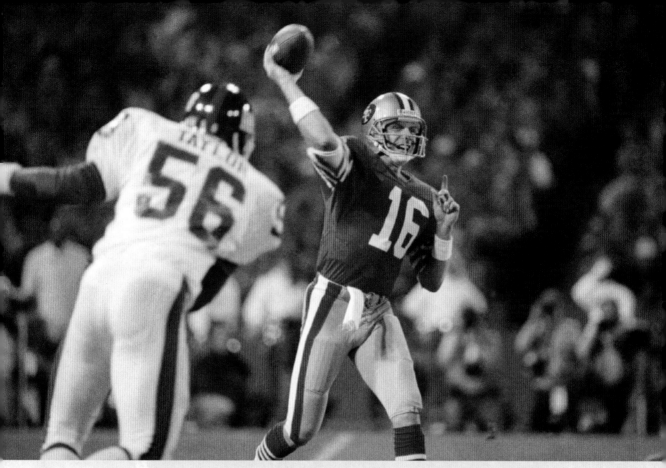

Playing in neighborhood football games as a child, Tom Brady always pretended to be Joe Montana, seen here during a game on December 1, 1986. AP PHOTO / PAUL SAKUMA

and each of Brady's three sisters would go on to earn collegiate scholarships for sports.

"I don't think we were typical girls," said Nancy. "We liked to play everything the boys did, and there were about eighty or ninety kids in the neighborhood, so there was always something going on. And it was always the three Brady girls and Tommy."

The kid brother reveled in the neighborhood games, but he was never the best player, or even close. "It's never come easy to me," he said. "I was always the one that no one ever picked. That's why I think I play with a chip on my shoulder. I have some scars that have never healed." When Brady did get picked to play, he struggled to keep up with the bigger kids. "He reached the height of the other boys' belly buttons," said Julie. "The older boys would mess with him, tell him to run deep and then never throw him the ball. He would trot back to the huddle flushed and perspiring, and tell them, 'I was open.' They would say, 'Go long again,' and run him ragged. He would return the next afternoon, ready to go again."

While Brady wasn't the fastest or most talented athlete, he was extremely competitive. "There was a kid in the neighborhood who was a lot faster than I was," he recalled. "I challenged him to a race. He killed me. I challenged him again. He killed me again. I just kept challenging him until I beat him. It's like the tortoise and the hare. I was the tortoise."

The stories about Brady being super-competitive are all true, and they started at a very young age. He was raised in an Irish Catholic household so competitive that arriving home from church on Sundays turned into a foot race. When the family car careened into the driveway, all four kids would spill out running, and whoever touched the front door first was the winner. "We used to compete for absolutely everything, and we pushed [Tommy] all the time," said Julie.

This attitude extended to their daily battles for control of the television remote. "My family had a rule: Whoever was the first person in the living room got to pick what they wanted to watch on TV," said Brady. "With three older sisters, you can imagine the fighting. It was always a rush, running downstairs or inside the house to be the first one to grab the remote. It was a free-for-all in the living room. We had some extreme pillow fights."

JOE COOL

In addition to being passionate participants in athletics, the Bradys were also fervent fans of the San Francisco 49ers. The family held season tickets during the best era in the franchise's history. The Niners won all five of their championships during the time Brady was in San Mateo. His favorite player was Hall of Fame quarterback Joe Montana.

On those autumn Sundays when the Niners were playing at home, as soon as the church service ended, the whole family was off to tailgate at Candlestick

Tom Brady's family was sitting in end-zone seats right behind where Dwight Clark made "The Catch" in the '81 NFC title game to beat Dallas. PETER READ MILLER VIA AP

Park, where Brady—dressed in a Joe Montana No. 16 jersey—threw a football around the stadium parking lot before going in to watch the game. Even though he did not play organized football until the ninth grade, Tommy showed a knack for tossing the pigskin. On a family outing during his middle school years, he won a bet against his dad by threading a pass through a tire 20 yards away. He then did it again. Tom Sr. was surprised to learn that his son had such a gift for throwing accuracy.

One of Brady's earliest football memories occurred when he was four years old, and his parents took him to Candlestick Park for the NFC Championship Game between the 49ers and the Dallas Cowboys, on January 10, 1982. The 49ers trailed that game by 6 points, with less than one minute to play. Six yards from a touchdown on third down, Montana took the snap under center and rolled out right. Desperate, and with three Cowboys bearing down on him, he heaved a pass to the back of the end zone that appeared to be hopelessly overthrown. There, Dwight Clark leapt high to make "The Catch," sending the 49ers to Super Bowl XVI. The crowd erupted in cheers, but Tommy cried, because his parents wouldn't buy him one of those oversized foam fingers that proclaimed the 49ers as being No. 1.

In the neighborhood football games that Brady played when he was older, he would always pretend to be Montana, and then, later, Steve Young, the left-handed quarterback and future Hall of Famer who eventually replaced Montana and who led the 49ers to the last of their five Super Bowl triumphs. "Every game we played, I was always Montana or Young, at least in my mind," said Brady, who also went to the 49ers Super Bowl victory parades in San Francisco. "The neighborhood driveways were my Candlestick Park."

"I was the one no one ever picked," said Brady. "That's why I play with a chip on my shoulder."

Brady also had posters of a couple of other Hall of Fame quarterbacks hanging on his bedroom wall, namely Denver Broncos great John Elway, who won two Super Bowls, and the Miami Dolphins' Dan Marino, who set numerous NFL passing records, but never won a Super Bowl. Marino did get one chance to shine on Super Sunday, but he ran into a red-hot Montana, who earned the big game's Most Valuable Player award for leading the 49ers past the Dolphins in Super Bowl XIX.

"Joe Montana, Steve Young, Jerry Rice—those were my heroes," Brady said. "Montana was the one I really looked up to. If there was anybody I could be like, it would be Joe Montana. No question."

Montana provided more than inspiration for Brady's football career. He also served as a role model for how Brady could attain greatness. Like Brady, Montana never possessed the elite athleticism that excites pro scouts. (The 49ers picked him in the third round of the 1979 draft.) But his knowledge of the game and his ability to perform under pressure led many to call Joe Cool the greatest of all time. He was the only player ever to earn Super Bowl MVP three times—until Tom Brady, who would do it five times.

"FIERCE AS A LION"

Although Brady's entire family enjoyed sports, his parents encouraged their kids to try all sorts of extracurricular activities, and introduced them to the fine arts by signing them up for piano, guitar, and dance lessons. But they all gravitated toward athletics, which led to the Brady kids participating in over three hundred sporting events a year. "We were kind of the ballpark, gym rat type of family," Brady Sr. said. There was a calendar in the kitchen that kept track of all their scheduled games, and mom and dad made sure that at least one parent attended every one. Brady always came along, and was his sisters' biggest cheerleader.

Losing never sat well with Brady, even when he was just the little brother trailing along to his sisters' softball and soccer games. Even then, the disappointing losses were tough to stomach—even if they weren't his. "They were the best athletes in my house, certainly better than I ever was," he said. "I just loved tagging along, and I was living and dying with every loss they had." Losses were few and far between, however, because Brady's sisters were accomplished athletes. In fact, before he was the greatest quarterback of all time—before he won more Super

Tom Brady and his father, Tom Sr., established a close relationship early on, spending Sundays golfing at the private club where the elder Brady was a member.
AP PHOTO / BEN MARGOT

Bowl MVPs than anybody in history—Tommy Brady was the fourth-best athlete in his own house.

Maureen, the oldest, was an All-American pitcher at Fresno State, compiling an 80-31 record and 0.98 earned run average in her college softball career. Julie started 72 games on the St. Mary's soccer team and earned second-team all–West Coast Conference honors as a senior. Nancy went to Cal to play softball, though she subsequently chose to pursue her studies. Brady's football career wouldn't truly surpass Maureen's achievements until he turned professional. That's why, for much of his life, Tom Brady was known as Tommy, Maureen's little brother.

Brady admired and supported his sisters, showing up to their games and cheering, but still, he always wanted to make a name for himself. In ninth grade, he wrote an essay in which he said that he hoped his siblings would one day be known as Tom Brady's sisters. Surrounded by accomplished athletes, he couldn't help developing the competitiveness that would become a driving force in his life. "My fault. I started it," admitted Tom Sr. "Everything we did, and I mean everything, like running home from church, throwing a rock the farthest—everything was a competition. I guess it made things really fun, at least for the winner."

Father and son established a close relationship early on, spending Sundays golfing at the private club where the elder Brady was a member. They'd go out and play at six-thirty in the morning and be home in time for church at eleven o'clock. To make things interesting, the Brady boys wagered side bets. The stakes were high: For every hole Tom Sr. won, Tommy promised to wash his car. For every hole Tommy won, his father would owe him a dollar. Brady never won any money, and due to washing all those cars, he developed an extreme distaste for losing. "Fierce as a lion," is how Julie described her little brother. "Call it what you want: strong-minded, hardheaded, determined. Tommy was all that. He would want to keep fighting until he won."

Although Brady's intense competitive fire is what pushed him to achieve success at every stage of his athletic career, it also, occasionally, sent him over the edge. There's still a small hole in the wall of the family room, a reminder of a long-ago temper tantrum, when in a fit of anger, he'd thrown the video game's remote controller. "I wound up breaking a TV and countless remotes," he admitted with a touch of embarrassment. "Finally, my mom just quit buying new ones for me."

Tommy Brady was the kid brother living in the shadows of his three older sisters.

When he was eleven years old, a frustrated Brady also lost his temper on the golf course after hitting a particularly bad shot during a father-son tournament. He slammed a club to the ground as hard as he could, which prompted his father to end the round on the spot and take him straight home. Tommy cried, and begged his father to bring him back to the course later that day to finish their nine holes. "I can lose it pretty good," said Brady. "That's not something I'm proud of, and I'd like to change it."

FAMILY BOND

Away from the playing fields, Brady kept his temper under control. He attended St. Gregory's School and was smart and popular, which didn't surprise the school's principal, Lorraine Paul, because "his older sisters were the same way." During these middle school years, he was similar to countless American boys at the time; he kept busy collecting baseball cards by the boxful, and made extra money as a paperboy. It was on his delivery route that Brady first demonstrated his arm strength, flinging newspapers from the back of his mother's Volkswagen

FAMILY VALUES

Brady's mom, Galynn, grew up on a dairy farm in Browerville, Minnesota, a small town with a population of 750 people. Though Tom and his three older sisters were raised in the San Francisco Bay Area, they visited their relatives, the Johnsons, on the farm in Browerville every summer as kids. It's where he worked the farm, fished, and picked up some old-fashioned Midwestern values.

Summer vacations spent in his mom's hometown created many a Minnesota memory, including the time Brady first tried chewing tobacco. During the car ride back to the farm from a family fishing trip, Brady asked his uncles if he could try some of their chewing tobacco. "[My uncles] said, 'Look, if we give [tobacco] to you, then you can't spit it out until you get home,' " Brady recalled. "And it was like a thirty-minute ride back to my grandpa's farm. So, of course, they give it to me, and within five minutes, I'm outside the car throwing up all over the place."

Galynn's brother, Allen Johnson, lives in the small white farmhouse that once belonged to his parents. He doesn't farm the land anymore, but rents out the pastures. Allen moved in to take care of Brady's grandfather, Gordon, before he died in 2016. Brady last visited Browerville in August 2016 to give a reading at the funeral.

van onto the neatly manicured lawns of the neighborhood. On Sunday mornings he played golf with his father, and then served his church as an altar boy. (His father had nearly become a priest before settling down and starting a family.)

Brady's parents made sure he and his sisters understood the values that would make the future NFL quarterback a fan favorite: Treat others well, and be humble. His parents were not teaching Brady these lessons so that he could one day handle his immense fame. They had no reason to believe their Tommy would one day become *the* Tom Brady. He was not a can't-miss athlete or a football prodigy. In fact, Brady's parents didn't allow their son to play tackle football until he entered high school, because they thought the sport was too dangerous for younger children. So he played other sports until high school, when his quarterbacking career would begin.

Like two of his sisters before him, Brady shined on the diamond and proved to be a solid, power-hitting catcher. The position he chose to play was facilitated by pedigree. When Brady Sr. was younger he was a catching prospect who was scouted by the Pittsburgh Pirates. Tommy dedicated most of his time to cultivating his baseball skills. Father and son would spend several days a week at the batting cages, and then go to a park, where Tommy would work on defense while his father hit him pop flies and ground balls.

Though Brady made his own mark and starred on the baseball field, his main motivation was simply to keep up with his

Tom Brady spent summer vacations in the Minnesota hometown of his mother, Galynn, seen here hugging her son in 2012.
AP PHOTO / MARK HUMPHREY

siblings, who were always the talk of the town. Even at a young age, Brady was determined to live up to the family name. "San Mateo isn't a big town, and his sisters were always the all-stars and the ones in the newspaper," said Tom Sr., recalling the formative years of his only son. "Being younger, he absorbed it; even if it came through osmosis, he picked up on it."

Brady also picked up on his siblings' drive to compete. "It was in our family's DNA to compete and want to win," he added. "My parents always encouraged that—to just go for it. It was great that my parents instilled that in me: You shoot for the stars and you try to do the best you can do."

SERRA HIGH SCHOOL, SAN MATEO

CHAPTER 2
DECISION TIME

TOM BRADY ATTENDED JUNIPERO SERRA HIGH SCHOOL, AN all-boys Catholic school located six blocks from his home, in San Mateo. Named for the man who brought Catholicism to California, Serra—as everyone who ever went there calls it—has sent a few of its graduates on to play professional baseball. Jim Fregosi, a shortstop with the California Angels, and later the manager of several major league teams, graduated from the school in 1959. And, almost a decade before Brady enrolled, the Serra Padres were led by a slugging outfielder named Barry Bonds, who went on to win seven National League Most Valuable Player awards with the Pittsburgh Pirates and San Francisco Giants, and set the Major League Baseball single-season record for home runs, with 73 in 2001, and then the career home-run record, in 2007. Although the school wasn't noted for turning out high-profile football players, there was one notable exception: Lynn Swann, the acrobatic wide receiver, who, after graduating in 1970, went off to the University of Southern California and then won four Super Bowl rings with the Pittsburgh Steelers between the 1974 and 1979 seasons, and was inducted into the Pro Football Hall of Fame in 2001.

Even though he had never before played a down of tackle football, Brady joined the Serra freshman football squad as a ninth grader in 1991, and with fantasies of becoming the next Joe Montana dancing in his head, set his sights on the quarterback position. He failed to win the starting job, and became the Padres' backup quarterback, suffering his first real athletic disappointment, worse than

Tom Brady eventually became a high school All-American quarterback who threw the ball convincingly enough to earn scholarship offers from several well-known football schools. SERRA HIGH SCHOOL, SAN MATEO

any family teasing. His parents didn't have to worry about him being injured, since he didn't take a single snap. He just sat on the bench and watched a Padres team that had zero wins, eight losses, and one tie. "That tells you how bad I was," considered Brady. "I couldn't crack the starting lineup of a team that didn't win a game."

Brady quickly learned just how much work he would have to put in to even get on the field. It was evident it wasn't going to be easy, so he practiced incessantly, trained during the off-season, and attended football camps in the summer. He wasn't all that great a player to begin with, but he had other desirable qualities: He was smart and tough, and he possessed a work ethic that some would call obsessive. Off the field, Brady was continually working hard to hone his game. "He hadn't shown any great promise as a football player at that point, but I just knew that, somehow, he would make it," recalled Rick Chandler, who coached Brady's ninth-grade team. "He was too smart, too positive, and loved football too much to not be successful. He just had that vibe."

Brady took over as the starting quarterback for junior varsity the following year, but only because the returning starter, his best friend, Kevin Krystofiak, had decided to quit the team and focus on basketball. Although he got to play only because he was the default option, he took advantage of the opportunity and started developing his quarterbacking skills. He passed accurately and effectively, connecting for 17 touchdown passes and only 3 interceptions, and was named to the first-team all-league junior varsity by the league's coaches.

> Brady couldn't crack the starting lineup on a team that didn't win a single game.

Despite achieving that level of success, Serra's head football coach, Tom MacKenzie, told Brady that he would have to work harder on his throwing mechanics and spend more time in the weight room if he wanted to make varsity next season. "I don't think I ever had to tell him to work hard again," said MacKenzie. "Because he didn't start out as a superstar, he learned how important it was to keep learning and growing as an athlete. He also learned that he would have to struggle if he wanted to reach his goals."

Brady responded to the coach's advice by working with a personal trainer and attending summer football camps. When he went to the camp run by Tom Martinez at the College of San Mateo, which he did for three years, Martinez worked with him on every aspect of what a quarterback should do, from how to drop back into the pocket to how to hold the football to throw with more accuracy. Brady impressed the noted quarterback guru with his attentiveness, even more than with his talent. "I've always said that people have two ears and one mouth, so they should listen twice as much as they talk," said Martinez. "But so many young kids don't want to listen. Tommy did. I'd talk, he would listen, and then he'd go and work at it. He worked his butt off and always believed in himself."

FIVE-DOT DRILL

Working hard was almost second nature to Brady, who always believed that increased effort leads to faster improvement. "I've always worked hard, and I've never minded doing it," he said. "I was always working on trying to improve my speed. During the summers I would run just as hard as I could. I would always come in last, but I would keep trying, and, eventually, I got a little bit faster and I also built up my stamina. I also lifted weights to increase the strength in my legs and my upper body. I did everything that I could to become the best quarterback that I could be."

Brady's throwing arm was never in question. ("He had a hell of an arm," an opposing high school coach later recalled. "He could throw it a mile.") Having grown to 6-foot-1 and 205 pounds, he also had excellent size.

His footwork and speed was another matter. His feet moved as if stuck in slabs of cement. Coach MacKenzie said he was one of the slowest players in high school, but also one of the smartest. "I've had better natural athletes than Tom Brady," he said. "But Tom Brady [was] my best football player." MacKenzie recognized an arm and the leadership skills that could succeed at the Division I college level. He also understood how much work it would take for the rest of Brady's game to catch up. MacKenzie frankly told Brady that to reach the next level, he needed to work below the waist. "That was all it took," said the coach. "Tom Brady is the only student-athlete I ever saw who took advantage of every opportunity that was provided to him."

MacKenzie created a workout program for his players called Bigger, Faster, Stronger. The most notorious of these workouts was the Five-Dot Drill. Coaches and teammates alike ridiculed Brady's foot speed when he lumbered and labored through the drill, which consists of five dots on a pad, arranged on the floor in a two-one-two fashion, like the five-dot side of a die. The goal is for players to hit each of the dots as fast as possible by jabbing with their feet in a staccato tempo at the marked spots using a number of variations. Players were timed as they went through certain patterns, like a fast version of hopscotch. It's a simple drill, but one that's perfect for building fast feet, balance, coordination, and agility. It can also wear you out in a hurry. "I've never been real fleet of foot,"

Tom Brady throwing the ceremonial first pitch at Boston's Fenway Park on April 13, 2015. The Montreal Expos (now the Washington Nationals) thought enough of his potential as a catcher to pick him in the eighteenth round of the 1995 baseball draft. AP PHOTO / ELISE AMENDOLA

Brady said. "I enjoyed the struggle of it. I gained a lot out of it, in terms of mental toughness."

Telling Brady that a quarterback didn't necessarily have to be a fast runner, but did need feet that were "quick in a phone booth," MacKenzie challenged Brady to improve his agility if he had hopes of winning a big-time college football scholarship. Brady participated in the training regimen set by the team, but took it upon himself to get better when no one was watching. He purchased a can of spray paint and created a template of the Five-Dot Drill on the Bradys' garage floor. He practiced the drill religiously, and became so adept at it that he even began creating his own unique variations. The workout had a dramatic effect on his speed and agility. Soon, he regularly logged some of the best times on the team. "Most teenagers will avoid at all cost what they aren't good at," said Coach MacKenzie. "Tom Brady was the opposite. He'd take to heart what he needed to improve on."

Brady relished the opportunity to improve his athleticism. He also invented his own jump-roping workout program and followed it fervently. MacKenzie asked him to write down the instructions and Junipero Serra football continues to use this same routine today. Brady became a jump-roping fanatic, not to mention a gym rat, and would leave his family's annual vacation in the Sierra Mountains to travel 40 miles to a gym so he could log the three-hour workout he did every day. Brady's obsessive behavior paid off. When he returned to Serra for his junior year, MacKenzie selected him as the varsity's starting quarterback.

The team started slowly; the Padres lost consecutive games by a combined score of 107–6. Brady took a pounding, but he didn't quit, and wouldn't allow his teammates to quit, either. Serra played on Fridays, reviewed game film on Saturdays, and Brady invited players to his home on Sundays to watch more film. His mom made everyone sandwiches while he'd tell his receivers where to break off routes and what everyone should be thinking, from play to play.

For the remainder of the season, he made very few mistakes, and seemed quick to read defenses and react to them. He soon discovered that he could make up in mechanics and film study what he lacked in natural gifts. The lanky junior had an effective, if not spectacular season; he led the Padres to a respectable 6-4 record and was named to the second-team all-county squad. "I was still very far from being a great quarterback, but I had definitely improved," he said.

"THAT *IT* FACTOR"

Back then, no one had a clue that Brady would win a college football scholarship, let alone go on to the NFL. In fact, his best sport was baseball, and he was a highly rated catching prospect. "At the time, I thought his future was in baseball," said Pete Jensen, Serra's baseball coach. "He could really throw." The kid could hit, too, and showed real ability as a powerful left-handed batter. He played two years of varsity baseball, 61 games in all, and batted .311 and had 8 home runs, 11 doubles, and 44 runs batted in. The coach remembers Brady hitting one monster home run in a playoff game that struck the team bus—parked well beyond the right-field fence—and waking the driver who was trying to take a nap. "Scared the heck out of him," the coach said.

Behind the plate, Brady was just as adept as a handler of pitchers, and like a true quarterback, he knew how to call a game. Coach Jensen let Brady call his own game—a luxury many college coaches don't afford their catchers—and Brady embraced the challenge. He would meet with pitchers before games and discuss strategy: how they were going to set up hitters and attack their weaknesses. Brady had played against many of these hitters in leagues growing up and knew their tendencies. "He had a book in his mind on these guys," said Jon Chapman, who pitched to Brady at Serra. "If I tried to shake him off, he'd throw down the same darn sign. It was like, 'Okay, we'll go with it. Tommy knows what he's doing.'"

By junior year, Brady, who had grown three inches, had become widely regarded as the top defensive catcher in the area, and started receiving recognition for his baseball talents. His teammates voted him captain, he was named to the all-county team, and scouts flocked to Serra to see him play. The Montreal Expos (now the Washington Nationals) became particularly interested in Brady after watching him hit a home run using a wooden bat during an open tryout at the Kingdome in Seattle.

When the Expos traveled to San Francisco to play the Giants in the spring, the major league club put Brady through a private workout at Candlestick Park—the very stadium where he had watched Joe Montana's heroics and fallen in love with football. He took batting practice and worked out behind the plate prior to the big-league game. "It was an impressive workout," said Kevin Malone, the Expos general manager. "He had a pretty good swing, and he had power. He was

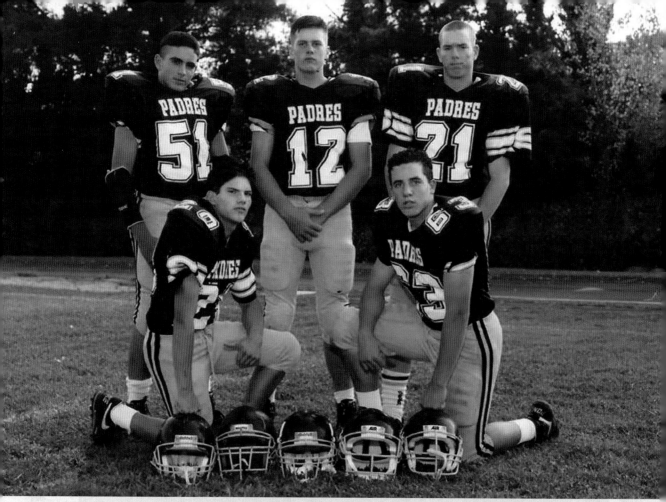

Even though he was near the top of his high school class and a highly touted athlete, Tom Brady (No. 12), according to a guidance counselor, was always just one of the guys. SERRA HIGH SCHOOL, SAN MATEO

not overwhelmed by the stadium or by hanging around major league players. He had poise. You wouldn't know—except for looking at his young face—that this guy was not part of our major league Montreal Expos team. He carried himself like a professional. He had that *it* factor."

Unbeknownst to baseball scouts, however, Brady was now moving decisively toward football as his primary sport. He loved the camaraderie of football and the team-oriented play that wasn't as prevalent on the baseball diamond. If he was going to win, he wanted it to be with his team; if they lost, he took it to heart. Brady was supremely passionate about the game of football—and about winning.

Kevin Donahue, Serra's athletic director, recalled Brady stewing in the end zone following a bitter loss to rival St. Francis. "He had tears in his eyes. He wasn't being a baby. He just hated to lose."

The hatred of losing, in many ways, is why Brady became a self-made star. After school, and after practice, and after homework, that time of the day when most teenagers are entranced by video games, Brady went to the nearby Pacific Athletic Club for an evening workout. His parents marveled at their son's hectic after-school schedule: Back home at 6:00 p.m., after football practice, he'd eat dinner and do homework until 7:30. Then he'd head to the gym and work out for a few hours, come back home, and do more homework until midnight. In addition to his performance on the field, Brady was a stellar student, accumulating a 3.5 average during his time at Serra. Even though he was near the top of his class and was a highly touted athlete, Tommy, according to a guidance counselor, was always just one of the guys.

Even as a popular student and the starting quarterback, playing in the football-saturated state of California did not mean instant glory. Serra was a mediocre team playing against some of the best teams in the country. Hoping to take advantage of Brady's talents, Coach MacKenzie tailored the Padres' offense to its star quarterback, using a spread system, which employs lots of receivers to give the passer options. Soon enough, Serra was scoring 30, 40 points a game, and college scouts took notice—not that they had a choice. Brady's father had sent out an extensive high-light tape of his son's best plays to over fifty college programs. The highlight package was split into different categories of throws—slants, screens, bombs, and fades—all set to generic '90s pop music. "I'd like to introduce my starting quarterback from this past season, Tom Brady," MacKenzie says in the video. "Tom is a 6-foot-4, 210-pound athlete that started all ten games for us this past season. He's a big, strong, very durable athlete, who has an excellent work ethic—especially in the off-season—and who does things to try to make himself a better athlete."

An MLB scout thought Brady "could have been one of the greatest catchers ever."

The video piqued the interest of California, Michigan, UCLA, USC, and Illinois, who promised to scout and evaluate Brady when his senior season began. That summer, in pursuit of his college football dream, Brady and his father visited football camps at colleges all over the West Coast. The trips provided solid father–son bonding time and gave Brady yet another opportunity to get the attention of schools with big-time college football programs.

One person whose attention Brady definitely got was Mike Riley, the offensive coordinator and quarterbacks coach for the University of Southern California. Riley had an eye for intangibles. He saw past Brady's shortcomings as an athlete—namely, his lack of mobility—and recognized a kid who read defenses and avoided mistakes; a kid who held the ball until the last possible moment, undaunted by pass rushers; and a kid whose team rallied around him. Riley was a constant presence at the summer football camps Brady attended, and trekked to San Mateo almost every week for a personal home visit. He soon developed a positive relationship with the quarterback and his family.

PLAYING IN THE TALL GRASS

Brady seemed to be leaning toward USC, which was apropos because, coincidentally, the Trojans' head coach, John Robinson, was a 1954 graduate of Serra High School. But then Riley got bad news from his boss: The team had already signed two quarterbacks, and no longer had a spot for Brady. Riley drove to San Mateo so he could break the bad news to Tom in person. Disappointed but unbowed, Brady entered his senior season with a strong arm and hard-earned and newfound athleticism. He was rated by national publications as one of the best quarterback prospects on the West Coast. His favorite high school receiver, John Kirby, could see and feel the difference in his QB's game. "Our senior year he threw me a 17-yard curl against Cardinal Newman," Kirby said. "As I turned around, I could hear the ball coming. It was making a hissing sound. It was like a missile."

Although the Padres—playing out of probably California's toughest league, the West Catholic Athletic League—finished with a mediocre 5-5 mark in Brady's senior season, he had made himself a big-time college prospect. He was selected first-team All-Northern California and was rated one of the top high school quarterbacks in the country by *Super Prep* magazine. *Blue Chip Illustrated* and *Prep Football Report* also recognized him as an All-American. He finished his high school career by completing 236 of 447 passes for over 3,500 yards and 31 touchdowns. That his record was just 11-9 as a two-year varsity starter, with no playoff appearances, did not stop dozens of colleges from trying to sign him. He threw the ball convincingly enough to earn scholarship offers from several well-known football schools. "I was lucky that I had choices coming out of high school, but I knew how hard I had worked to be in that position," said Brady. "I already had the size and arm strength, so I knew that if I worked hard enough and dedicated myself to playing, that I could make it."

Brady soon narrowed down his choice to three schools—Michigan, California, and Illinois—with academics playing a major factor in his decision. His father hoped that his son would choose Cal and stay close to the family. As such, Cal felt they were front-runners for Brady's services. That changed during a recruiting visit to Ann Arbor, when Brady privately decided he wanted to be a Michigan man. They played in the Big 10 Conference, and the football program had an undeniable historic aura. He wanted to lead the Wolverines onto the field at The Big House in front of 110,000 screaming fans dressed in maize and blue. He wanted to walk down State Street after the game as the Michigan quarterback, the big man on campus. "I loved the social aspect. I loved the team. It was a great school," he said. "It was more of a feeling. Once I experienced that, I really didn't want to go anywhere else."

Although Brady's heart had settled on football, big-league baseball scouts continued to monitor his progress on the diamond. With the Major League Baseball draft fast approaching, it seemed likely that an MLB team would select him. But

The dream of leading the Michigan Wolverines onto the field at The Big House in front of 110,000 screaming fans was appealing to Brady.
AP PHOTO / PAUL WARNER

there was one major issue: Brady had indicated that football was his true love, and that he planned on attending college in the fall. If that were the case, drafting him would be useless. Kevin Malone, the general manager of the Montreal Expos, decided to take a chance anyway, and thought enough of Brady's potential as a backstop to pick him in the eighteenth round of the 1995 baseball draft, No. 507 overall. "I think he could have been one of the greatest catchers ever," Malone has said.

Now Brady had a decision to make. He'd have to choose football or baseball. He had his mind set on playing football, and he turned the Expos down. Ultimately, the Montreal players helped to convince Brady to play football, asking him during his workout at Candlestick Park why he'd choose the tough life of a minor league baseball player over the fun of being a football star at a large university.

Once he had decided on football over baseball, one big decision remained. Michigan or California? The Brady family gathered in their living room in San Mateo. Tom broke the bad news to his father: He was going to commit to Michigan, not to Cal. "I was crying like a baby and said, 'Tommy, this is going to change our relationship,' " said Tom Sr. "And he said: 'Dad, I know. It has to.' " A few days later, the Wolverines head coach, Gary Moeller, flew out to San Mateo to close the deal. Tom Brady signed a letter of intent to play football at the University of Michigan. Some of Brady's high school coaches wondered if he should have taken the safer, closer option at Cal-Berkeley, or pursued a baseball career, but Brady fell in love with Ann Arbor, much to the dismay of his father, who was distraught that his only son would be playing some 2,100 miles from home. In retrospect, however, Brady's father should have known that Tommy wanted the big time. Under his picture in his high school yearbook, Brady wrote: "If you want to play with the big boys, you gotta learn to play in the tall grass."

Brady still looks back with great fondness at the years he spent at Serra. "I had a wonderful time in high school," he said. "I went to a great school, with tremendous academic support, a darned good baseball team, and a pretty good football team. Going there helped me a lot when I started college." The young quarterback was leaving California, but he wouldn't soon be forgotten. The trophy case at Serra High School displays a *Sports Illustrated* magazine with Brady's face on the cover, and his high school football jersey hangs from the ceiling of the gymnasium. Next to his name he signed an autograph with the inscription "SB 36, SB 38 MVP"—a reference to his first two NFL championship wins. It hangs near those of two other former Padres legends: Lynn Swann and Barry Bonds.

Brady has remained closely connected to his alma mater. He donated the Cadillac truck he won as the MVP of Super Bowl XXXVIII to the school. The ensuing raffle raised more than $340,000 for renovations. The school tried renaming the football venue in his honor a few years ago. Brady was touched, but told school officials that the key to his Serra experience was how hard his parents had worked to send him there in the first place. So at the quarterback's suggestion, Padres games are now played at Brady Family Stadium. For all he had done, and for all he would do, Tom Brady will forever be the pride of San Mateo.

CHAPTER 3
MICHIGAN MAN

HANGING ON A WALL IN THE LOCKER ROOM AT MICHIGAN STA-dium is a sign that reads: THOSE WHO STAY WILL BE CHAMPIONS. It is the motto of Michigan football.

While Tom Brady Sr. let his son make his own decision about where to attend college, he was distraught when his son selected Michigan over Cal-Berkeley, which is just 35 miles across the San Francisco Bay from the Brady home in San Mateo. Father and son were best friends, and Brady Sr. worried about the separation. More disheartening, by the time Tom Brady arrived at Ann Arbor to start his college career at Michigan in the summer of 1995, the coach who had recruited him and the head coach, Gary Moeller, who had approved the scholarship, were no longer at Michigan. Moeller had been fired, and his replacement, Lloyd Carr, was the defensive coordinator, and Brady didn't know him.

Brady's first football practice didn't make him feel any better, because he discovered he was at the bottom of the team's quarterback depth chart, behind six other talented signal callers. The Wolverines were so stocked at the position that Carr, the new head coach, decided to redshirt Brady, which meant that he could practice with the team but he could not play at all in his freshman year at Michigan. He spent the year working out, watching film, studying film, and practicing.

"Nobody who I had established a relationship with was there, and I felt like a bit of an orphan," said Brady, who had just turned eighteen and was over 2,000

Tom Brady (No. 10, second row, center) sat on the bench for a Michigan team coached by Lloyd Carr that won the national championship in 1997. AP PHOTO / CARLOS OSORIO

miles away from his family, living on his own for the first time in his life. "It was certainly a growing-up experience, and I learned that I'd better grow up quickly."

Far from being a prized recruit, Brady returned to Ann Arbor in 1996, in what was his freshman season of athletic eligibility, determined to prove himself. What made the situation even more daunting was that the players in front of him were Scott Dreisbach, who was only one year ahead of Brady, and Brian Griese, who was two years ahead of him. Brady wondered if he'd made the wrong decision by not going to a different school, one where he wouldn't be at the end of the line. "I wasn't in a very good position," noted Brady, who began working as hard as he could to improve his game, and his ranking. "It's not as though they were graduating seniors. I didn't have much of a chance unless one of those guys got hurt or I improved."

Although Brady was relegated to playing with the third team in practice, he began to make an impression. "He was running with the second and third groups, playing behind guys that couldn't block me and you," said Stan Parrish, Brady's quarterback coach for four years in Ann Arbor. "They kept knocking him down and he'd get up and keep competing." During the season, Brady picked up meaningless garbage time as the Wolverines' third-string quarterback. He played in only two games, completing 3 of 5 passes, for a total of 26

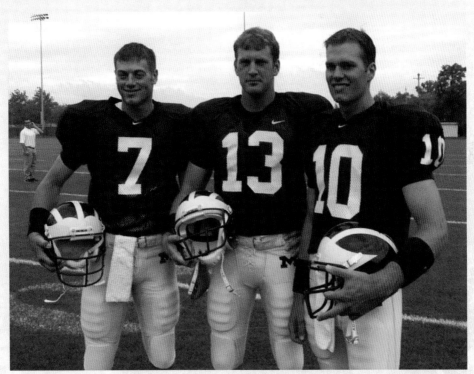

Tom Brady (10) waged an annual battle to be Michigan's starting quarterback. He vied for the position against Drew Henson (7) and Jason Kapsner (13) in 1999. AP PHOTO / CARLOS OSORIO

yards. The first pass he ever threw as a college quarterback was to a UCLA linebacker who brought it all the way back for a touchdown. It was a humbling experience. "I thought I had improved enough to play, but in looking back I realize that I wasn't ready at that point," said Brady. "There's so much more that goes into being a quarterback than throwing the football. You also need to have leadership skills, poise, and concentration. It's a learning process; at least, it was for me."

CAREER CROSSROADS

With a determination that first manifested itself in the Five-Dot Drill back in high school, Brady continued to hit all the marks on improving himself. Still, it wasn't enough. In 1997, at that year's spring camp, Brady once again found himself slotted in behind the backup, Scott Dreisbach, and the starter, Brian Griese, whose father, Bob, had been the star quarterback for the two-time Super Bowl champion Miami Dolphins.

The three-man competition at the spring camp was ferocious. The coaches and players were struck by Brady's willingness to hang in the pocket until the precise moment the ball needed to be thrown. "They kept blitzing him and he kept standing in there and throwing the ball right on the money," Carr recalled.

Brady thought of transferring; he felt stymied, his talents underappreciated.

"He got beat up pretty good, and you could tell he was really competitive and real tough." Brady clearly jumped ahead of Dreisbach on the depth chart, and came tantalizingly close to beating out Griese as the Wolverines' starter. "When we broke camp, it was neck and neck between the two of them," said Stan Parrish, the team's quarterbacks coach. "You could have almost flipped a coin." But when Griese was designated the Michigan starter, Brady was devastated.

Brady was frustrated because he felt as though he deserved to start, and expressed that thought to his coach. Carr told him to quit worrying about other guys and to worry only about himself. His father, too, told him he wasn't going to win by taking on the head coach; he could only take on himself.

Brady began to think he might be stymied at Michigan, and his talents under-appreciated by the head coach. He decided to talk to Carr once again and express how he felt. When he met with Carr, he admitted that he was thinking of transferring to California-Berkeley to play quarterback and to be closer to his family. Carr understood his rationale, but told him to sleep on the decision. Brady agonized over it. "I really wasn't sure where my career was going to go," he said. "I just wasn't sure if I would ever get an opportunity to play."

Remembering the Michigan football motto, he decided not to quit. *Those who stay will be champions.* As he promised, Brady went back the next day to see Carr in his office. This time, Brady said with confidence, "I've decided I'm going to stay at Michigan, and I'm going to prove to you I'm a great quarterback." Brady then did something that seemed extreme at the time. Just as he had hired a personal trainer when he needed to bulk up in high school, he sought out a sports psychologist to help him reach optimal mental strength. From the psychologist, he learned how to worry less about factors out of his control, and to focus more on what he could control. "Honestly," said Carr, "from that day forward he was relentless in the pursuit of proving who he was."

Given the chance to start, Brian Griese took advantage of his opportunity and went on to lead the Wolverines to an undefeated 12-0 season, which he capped with an MVP performance in the Wolverines' 21–16 win over Washington State in the Rose Bowl. The Associated Press declared Michigan the national football champion for the first time since 1948. Brady appeared in only four games in mop-up duty as Griese's backup that season, completing 12 of 15 passes for 103 yards. An emergency appendectomy had ended his season in October. He wound up losing 30 pounds. He was sick, and emotionally battered. "That was the low point," said teammate Scot Loeffler. "But those hard times paid off. From then on, he just decided that he was going to be our starting quarterback."

Tom Brady led Michigan to a 10-2 record in 1999, including a come-from-behind win over Penn State in State College, Pennsylvania.

OPPORTUNITY KNOCKS

Brady may have decided to stay at Michigan, but his talk with Carr didn't produce an immediate change in his situation. The only statistics Brady had to show after his first two seasons were 15 passes completed (out of 20 attempts) for 129 yards, an interception, and two rushing attempts for negative 14 yards. He was still a long way from playing, but his attitude had changed. He was out to win practice every day. He had committed to staying at Michigan. He wanted to prove to Carr that he was the best option at quarterback. As he always did, Brady kept pressing in pursuit of fulfilling his dream. Teammates who lived with Brady could hear him leaving at six o'clock in the morning to go work out, and marveled at how he could watch game film late into the night.

"When he was second or third on the depth chart, he was still studying film at 10:30, 11 at night," said Pat Kratus, a roommate and teammate. "He was frustrated with not playing, and that's how he channeled it. Whenever you talked to him about the future, he was adamant: 'I'm going to be a starting quarterback in the NFL.' He always had confidence in his own success. It wasn't braggadocio. That was just his plan from the word 'go.'"

In the spring and summer of 1998, preparing for his junior season of football, Brady, after regaining his strength, fully expected to be the Michigan starter. The path was clear. Griese, a third-round pick of the Denver Broncos, was gone from Ann Arbor. Brady had sat for three years, but now he finally had his chance. In the fall, Brady won the battle with Scott Dreisbach for the starting role. But his hold on the reins was tentative, because lurking in the wings was a freshman phenomenon named Drew Henson, who many people, including coach Lloyd Carr, thought was the next great Michigan quarterback. "Obviously, Brady has an advantage because he's paid his dues," said Carr, in what was an underwhelming show of support. "But there's no question that Henson is the most talented quarterback ever to come to Michigan."

> "He's not the greatest athlete, but I think he's the smartest guy going, and he's a great leader."
> —BOB GRIESE, HALL OF FAME QB

Drew Henson was a three-sport star from nearby Brighton, Michigan, 19 miles from Ann Arbor. He was a local hero with an astonishing high school career who came along just when Brady had ascended to first string. As an unbelievable athlete in football, baseball, and basketball, Henson was everything Brady wasn't—a can't-miss talent who had been the subject of a profile in *Sports Illustrated* magazine, and had already signed a contract with the New York Yankees for $2 million to play minor league baseball only during the summers.

Carr named Brady the starter, but the coach immediately said the golden-boy freshman would also get to play. Henson probably was Michigan's most heralded in-state football recruit in history, so there was tremendous pressure on Carr to elevate the local hero over Brady. Although he knew that his hold on the job might be tenuous, and that Carr could turn to Henson in a heartbeat, Brady had no intention of yielding what he had waited so long to achieve. "To be the best, you have to beat out the best," he said. "I've fought long and hard to be in this position, and I don't plan to give it up."

SHARING THE SPOTLIGHT

Brady got off to a shaky start as a fourth-year junior in 1998, and the Wolverines, who had come into the season ranked No. 5 in the nation, struggled in defense of their national championship. Michigan dropped its first two games, 36–20 at Notre Dame, and then a 38–28 spanking by Syracuse, before 111,012 disappointed fans in Ann Arbor.

In each of those two games, Henson had come in to mop up, and he wound up generating more offense than Brady had. In fact, it was the freshman that had come into the Syracuse game in the fourth quarter, and then proceeded to pilot the Wolverines to three of their four touchdowns. Adding insult to injury, when Brady threw an interception early in the Syracuse game and was immediately benched by Carr, the Michigan Stadium fans cheered when Henson ran onto the field. The fans wanted Henson to be the starter.

For the rest of that year, Brady would hear boos when he played poorly, and people would call for his benching. "In regard to being pulled from the games, I can only control what I control, which is how I play," said Brady. "When Coach decides to put Drew in the game, I have to deal with that. When I do get called on to come in after Drew, I have to go out there and perform." That is exactly what Brady did, as he led the Wolverines to wins in 10 of their final 11 games, including a 45–31 come-from-behind win over Arkansas in the Citrus Bowl.

Brady's play seemed to impress

Tom Brady played the game of his life in the Orange Bowl against the Alabama Crimson Tide, on January 1, 2000.
AP PHOTO / *DETROIT NEWS*, DANIEL MEARS

his head coach, and made him look like a lock to return as the starter for his senior season. "Tom's a bright guy, he has a good arm, and his teammates look up to him," said Carr. "I think he has the right stuff." By the following autumn, however, Carr had decided that Brady, who had been elected one of the team's captains, would start the opening game and Henson would play the second quarter. Then, at halftime, Carr would decide whom to send in to start the second half. The pattern would repeat itself over and over again throughout the season. Most football observers believed the system Carr had devised, ostensibly to keep both quarterbacks happy, was guaranteed to please neither of them. "I don't think either one of them was happy with it," Carr recalled. "Tom, as a captain and a fifth-year senior, clearly, it was tougher on him."

It was a tough situation indeed, especially for a senior who was down to his last season and his final attempt to progress as a player and attract the attention of NFL scouts. But Brady never pouted or grumbled about the decision. "I'm not saying whether or not he liked it, but Tom never flinched, never complained," said Mike DeBord, the Wolverines' offensive coordinator. "He was handed a difficult situation and he handled it beautifully."

While Brady privately bristled at the way coach Carr treated him, he kept his concerns largely to himself. "There's no question," added DeBord, "he could've blown up the team." Instead, he went on being a model teammate, grinding in the film room, and staying positive in the wake of feeling jerked around.

Starter or backup, win or lose, his family's support never wavered.

"The way I looked at it," Brady said, "I was getting a chance to play, which I hadn't had my first two years. All I wanted was the opportunity, and I still had that. All I wanted was the chance to play, and to share some camaraderie, to share some memories with so many other guys."

Starter or backup, win or lose, his family's support never wavered. Brady's parents traveled around the country to Tommy's games, trading in the short neighborhood commute of his childhood to a wealth of frequent-flyer miles. As always, his sisters continued to cheer him on—albeit, from a distance. "It was just great to grow up in a house like that and feel so supported by your mom and dad," he said. "I've always had that great support at home. I certainly wouldn't be standing here if I didn't have the love and support of my parents and my sisters and my family."

QUARTERBACK CAROUSEL

The Wolverines opened their 1999 schedule against Notre Dame for the second straight year, but this time Brady turned the tables on the Fighting Irish by rallying Michigan from a 3-point deficit in the final ninety seconds to win, 26–22. Brady started against Notre Dame, but Henson replaced him in the second quarter, receiving an enormous cheer from Michigan fans. Henson completed 3 of

6 passes for 40 yards, but Carr put Brady back into the game early in the third quarter. Brady was booed. "I think we're way beyond that," Brady said afterwards, of being booed. "We just know we have to go out and execute."

Carr continued to rotate his quarterbacks for the next six games. It was a surreal juggling experiment. Every time Henson took the field, he got an ovation from the local fans. For most of the season as Michigan's starter, Brady dealt with the ever-looming specter of Henson, knowing that one mistake at the wrong time could cost him. But Brady played well enough to be tapped as the second-half starter in all of the games, and the Wolverines' record stood at 5-0, having kicked off the season by beating Notre Dame, Rice, Syracuse, Wisconsin, and Purdue—a game in which Brady and Michigan snapped the Boilermakers' 10-game winning streak with Drew Brees under center. It was only a matter of time before Brady would eventually outplay Henson and send the youngster back to the bench for good. "He never backed down from a challenge," said DeBord, the UM offensive coordinator. "That's the thing that always impressed me about Tom."

In the sixth week, Michigan played Michigan State, their in-state rival from just up the road in East Lansing. For this game, Carr changed the pattern of his quarterback carousel, starting Brady in the first half and Henson in the second. Henson threw an interception that put Michigan down, 27–10, and, in the fourth quarter, Carr brought Brady back in to try to salvage the game. Brady nearly pulled Michigan all the way back—he threw for 241 yards in the final eighteen minutes—but despite his best effort to mount a comeback, the Wolverines suffered their first loss of the season, 34–31. Carr stayed with this scheme for one more game, a 35–29 loss to Illinois in Ann Arbor. Henson again made a critical error while Brady threw for 307 yards, further separating himself from the sophomore challenger. Afterward, it was announced that Brady would be Michigan's first-team quarterback for the rest of the season. Carr finally gave

"I've got a ton of respect for Tom and what he's accomplished. I don't know if there is a guy in this game that is more disciplined, more mentally tough and [as] consistent."

—DREW BREES

Brady his full endorsement, and only then did he have the job security not to have to look over his shoulder.

After Carr finally stopped the merry-go-round and put the team entirely in his fifth-year senior's hands, Brady would never lose another game in college. With Brady at the wheel, Michigan rode to four straight wins, coming from behind in the last two of them—a tough 31–27 win at Penn State, and a victory at home, 24–17, over archrival Ohio State—to end the regular season with a 10-2 record. Brady's resolve had been severely tested, but the twenty-two-year-old ultimately proved he was equal to the task. "Nothing was given to him," said Parrish, the UM quarterbacks coach. "He earned everything he got."

Tom Brady finished his college career in a blaze of glory, completing 34 of 46 pass attempts for 369 yards and 4 touchdowns, to lead Michigan to a 35–34 overtime win against Alabama in the Orange Bowl. He had engineered the kind of pressure-packed, comeback victory he would soon accomplish so often in the NFL. It was an inspirational triumph, an entire team effort. "Everyone felt that way, that they wouldn't give up," Brady said. "I was counting on everybody else, and they were counting on me. What a great way to go out as a fifth-year senior."

Brady had played the game of his life, and the most prolific game by a quarter-back in school history. However, the Most Outstanding Player award went to his primary target that day, sophomore wide receiver David Terrell, who caught 10 passes for 150 yards and 3 touchdowns. "He [Brady] won this game," Terrell said moments after the victory. "Tom Brady showed poise. He showed the heart of a leader, the heart of a lion."

After the Orange Bowl triumph, as was the custom, Michigan's team captains led their adoring fans in singing a chorus of "The Victors," the Wolverines' fight song. Brady's voice could be heard clearly above the rest. As the Michigan players and coaching staff celebrated the cathartic victory, Stan Parrish sought out Brady's parents amid the pandemonium. What their son had gone through,

Tom Brady leads adoring fans in a chorus of the Michigan fight song after an Orange Bowl triumph.
AP PHOTO / *DETROIT NEWS*], DANIEL MEARS

Parrish told them, would have broken most players. "That's what Brady is all about, and that's what Michigan is all about," said the coach. "He's a special guy."

In retrospect, college was a valuable proving ground for Brady. He had come to Michigan as an untested seventh-stringer, but he left as one of the top quarterbacks in the school's history. And through those five years of growth, as difficult as the process had often been, he learned that he could, indeed, play in the tall grass with the big boys.

Although Tom Brady won a national championship in 1997 as a backup quarterback, and later led Michigan to dramatic bowl victories over Arkansas and Alabama in his two years as a starter, he was underrated and underestimated during his entire college career. It's hard to figure out why Brady was never shown the love he deserved at Michigan until he was ready to leave, but he holds no grudges. "It was a great learning experience for me," he said. "Everyone has their own journey, and my journey was a very competitive one. I was forced to compete on a daily basis. It wasn't, 'Okay, if you commit to Michigan, you're going to be the quarterback your second year.' And that's probably how a lot of kids want it, you know? They didn't promise me anything." In the end, even Lloyd Carr had come to appreciate the fact that Brady had not only achieved athletic success, but that he had done so with dedication and determination. "He made believers out of everybody here," said the coach. "He represents everything that's positive about being an athlete."

"You're synonymous now with Babe Ruth, with Michael Jordan. The university that he attended should build a statue."
—JIM HARBAUGH,
MICHIGAN COACH

Tom Brady was finally appreciated as a Michigan man. Two weeks after the thrilling Orange Bowl victory, he returned to California for the East-West Shrine Bowl, and performed well in the college football all-star game at Stanford Stadium, near his hometown of San Mateo. Playing before his neighbors for the first time while wearing a Michigan helmet, he threw two touchdown passes for the winning East side. Brady was winding down his college career, and hoping that his future would include some time in the National Football League. "I certainly believe, with the way I've progressed over the years, I can play at the next level," he said before the East–West Shrine Bowl. "Will I? It depends on a lot of things. You've got to be in the right place at the right time."

As it turned out, Tom Brady would make a career of being in the right place at the right time.

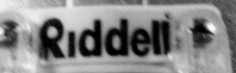

CHAPTER 4
UNDERRATED AND UNDERESTIMATED

IN THE WINTER OF 1999, TOM BRADY LEFT THE UNIVERSITY OF Michigan with a degree in general studies, with an emphasis in business administration. He played well in the college football all-star game back home in California. After the season, when Michigan hosted pro scouts at its annual Pro Day, Brady came to the attention of Dick Rehbein, the quarterbacks coach of the New England Patriots. Rehbein and his new boss, head coach Bill Belichick, were looking for someone to back up Drew Bledsoe, the franchise quarterback who'd led the Patriots to a Super Bowl appearance three years earlier.

Dick Rehbein had sharpened his football coaching teeth under Bart Starr, who lived up to his name as the quarterback of Vince Lombardi's dynastic Green Bay teams that won five NFL titles during the 1960s, including the first two Super Bowls. Starr was not a great athlete, but he was noted for his ability to make clutch plays at big moments. He also was the Packers head coach from 1975 to 1983. While Starr was coaching Green Bay, he hired Rehbein as the special teams coordinator.

Now, more than a decade later, as Patriots quarterbacks coach, Rehbein went to Ann Arbor looking for a player he could mold into a durable backup quarterback. He watched Brady perform position-specific drills, and came away thinking the Michigan standout threw the ball accurately and had greater arm

The Patriots scouted Tom Brady and liked what they saw: a smart young man who worked hard, and to whom players seemed to respond.
AP PHOTO / SCOTT BOEHM

strength than one might guess by looking at him. Rehbein talked to Wolverines players about Brady, and gradually, a professional profile of the young quarterback began to emerge.

From teammates, Rehbein learned that Brady showed up at Michigan as a seventh-stringer. He didn't transfer after losing a tight quarterback battle to Brian Griese. Instead of complaining about having to split snaps with freshman Drew Henson simply because Henson was a heralded recruit, Brady proved how much better he was than his backup, and ended up winning the starting job. The New England coach also liked what he was hearing about Brady from the Michigan coaches. That he routinely led Michigan on clutch game-winning drives. That he was a smart young man who worked hard, and whom players seemed to respond to. He was, by all accounts, the leader of the Wolverines' locker room. He also produced what coaches refer to as "good tape," and checked all of the boxes when it came to intangibles. Everything pointed to Brady becoming a good NFL quarterback and a great leader. Rehbein came away convinced that he had found more than a backup: He'd found a diamond in the rough—perhaps the next Bart Starr.

THE EYE TEST

While Rehbein began touting him in New England, Brady traveled to a sports performance clinic in Metairie, Louisiana, to train and to further improve his foot speed and agility. Then he went off to the NFL Scouting Combine in Indianapolis, a weeklong showcase dedicated to measuring the prospective draftees, from their speed in the 40-yard dash to their intellectual and emotional ability to play the game professionally. Brady scored high on those portions of the aptitude test concerned with organization, leadership, intelligence, commitment, character, and attitude. But Brady's on-field performance at the 2000 NFL Combine was horrendous.

Never a fast runner, Brady was clocked in a snail-like time of 5.28 seconds in the 40-yard dash, and recorded an abysmal 24.5-inch vertical jump, third worst of *any* player at that year's Combine, and the worst for a quarterback in nearly thirty-five years. In the standing broad jump, Brady recorded a leap of 99 inches that would've ranked dead last among quarterbacks at the 2019 NFL Scouting Combine. While seasoned scouts will tell you that game tape is king, how a prospect performs at the NFL Combine will echo on Draft Day—whether they like it or not. A wide receiver may pass the eye test on film in the autumn, but if he runs a tenth of a second too slow in the 40-yard dash—the Combine's main event—his stock will almost certainly fall in the eyes of teams' general managers, scouts, and coaches. It's that important. It's all or nothing, with all the marbles on the line.

Tom Brady didn't exactly look like a burgeoning star at the 2000 NFL Combine, and he certainly didn't wow anyone with his physical stature. Of the numerous enduring images from his glittering, Super Bowl–laden career, perhaps the most striking of all is one that came right at the very beginning. He has long been mocked and ridiculed for an unflattering photograph taken at the Combine. Today, the NFL Network, which broadcasts virtually every aspect of the workouts, won't show guys in their skivvies jumping on a scale to be weighed. They say it makes the players uncomfortable. Maybe they're still freaked out by the sight of Brady from 2000, looking more like a nerdy algebra student than a future Super Bowl winner. Standing in dreary gray gym shorts, shirtless, with nothing resembling muscle definition, pasty-white arms drooping at his side, shoulders slumped, the twenty-two-year-old Brady looked a million miles from the future Hall of Fame, multiple MVP-winning quarterback he has become. A future husband to a Victoria's Secret model he certainly was not. NFL scouts were understandably skeptical about his professional future.

One NFL draft pundit said Brady "didn't have the total package of skills" to play on Sundays.

Although Brady had gained a reputation as a determined and intelligent player, after turning in one of the worst Combine performances ever recorded by a quarterback prospect, the buzz on Brady faded. He was labeled as a middling

Bill Belichick liked the way Tom Brady would get thrown into games and lead the Wolverines back to victory, including this win against Michigan State in 1998. AP PHOTO / PAUL WARNER

prospect who lacked any exceptional physical skills. The scouting report on him was filled with negatives: "Poor build. . . . Skinny. . . . Lacks great physical stature and strength. . . . Lacks mobility and ability to avoid the rush. . . . Lacks a really strong arm. . . . Can't drive the ball downfield. . . . Does not throw a really tight spiral. . . . System-type player who can get exposed if forced to ad lib. . . . Gets knocked down easily."

Fortunately, Dick Rehbein wasn't deterred by Brady's woeful performance and pathetic appearance at the pre-draft NFL Combine. Nothing dissuaded him from believing in Brady. The positives were few, but to Rehbein, they were a better indicator of Brady's potential. "Very poised and composed. . . . Produces in big spots and in big games. . . . Team leader."

Now the quarterbacks coach needed to convince his boss, Bill Belichick, that Brady was worth a pick. Rehbein pointed out that, among Brady's other attributes, Michigan had won 20 of 25 games under his direction, and he had engineered come-from-behind postseason victories in back-to-back bowl games.

> "You saw that body [at the 2000 NFL Combine]. There's no way you saw [seven] championships in that body!"
>
> —MICHAEL IRVIN,
> HALL OF FAME WIDE RECEIVER

Belichick listened to Rehbein's glowing assessment of Brady, and made a call to Michigan head coach Lloyd Carr. Despite his early misgivings, Carr said, he had become a true believer in Brady, who expressed some traits that could not be measured in a 40-yard dash—especially his toughness. "I told [the Patriots] that they'd never regret drafting him, and that Tom had every intangible you could ask for," Carr recalled.

RED FLAG

Although Tom Brady eventually established himself as one of the top passers in Michigan history, and had also shown that he had the mental toughness to thrive in the midst of a difficult situation, NFL teams were less than overwhelmed with his potential in professional football. Several teams, including the Buffalo Bills, questioned Brady's abilities by citing, among other things, the fact that he had had trouble at the outset finding his place at Michigan. "The big question that scouts had on him was why Michigan would try to play a freshman over him," said Tom Donahoe, the general manager of the Buffalo Bills. "That had everybody concerned."

The doubts went so deep that many draft pundits, including the most famous of them, Mel Kiper Jr., commented that Brady "didn't have the total package

The long wait on Draft Day was emotionally draining for Brady, who grew anxious as other players were being selected ahead of him. AP PHOTO / SCOTT BOEHM

of skills" to play on Sundays. Following Brady's unremarkable performance at the NFL Combine, a flock of quarterbacks hurdled ahead of him on teams' draft lists. Some teams, such as the Patriots, thought Brady still might be worth a shot. Other teams, including the San Francisco 49ers, his hometown team, didn't. Brady participated in a local combine for San Francisco head coach Steve Mariucci and the team's special advisor, the legendary Bill Walsh, but failed to impress the man who'd drafted Joe Montana, Tommy Brady's idol. Mariucci, too, was uninterested. "You saw this tall, gangly kid [who] looked like he'd never seen a weight room," said Mariucci, who also was unimpressed with Brady's throwing ability. "There were some other guys that could shoot it, and he had just an okay arm."

Dick Rehbein continued to push for the Patriots to draft Brady, and in New England, they were listening. Bill Belichick's father, Steve, had been a coach and a scout, and he'd educated his son about the importance of a player's intangibles. Still, if Carr valued Brady's toughness, why did he insist on platooning him with Henson during his senior season? Belichick had a hard time wrapping his head around that question. "You say, okay, they don't really want this guy as their starting quarterback. They want another guy. What's the problem here? It was a bit of a red flag," Belichick told NFL Films in 2011. Another issue was the team's relative stability at the quarterback position. When Belichick took over the team a few months prior, the Patriots already had three quarterbacks under contract: the twenty-eight-year-old Drew Bledsoe, veteran backup John Friesz, and third-stringer Michael Bishop.

"We didn't open up his chest and look at his heart. What kind of spine he had. And resiliency, and all the things that are making him really great right now."

—STEVE MARIUCCI, EX-NFL COACH

The Patriots really didn't need to draft another quarterback. But Belichick was shrewd enough to eventually come around and see Lloyd Carr's experiment as a point to be taken in Brady's favor. Belichick particularly liked Brady's mental toughness and the way he would get thrown into games and lead the Wolverines back to victory. "There was nothing we could do about the whole Henson situation," the coach added. "We just had to evaluate what we saw. And we saw Tom time and again his senior year start the game off well, and then so many times Tom would come back in and rescue the situation and pull out the win for Michigan against great competition, in the biggest game. He just took his opportunities and tried to make the most of them."

New England's third-year fullback, Chris Floyd, had been lifting weights before the draft when Belichick asked him about Brady, his former Michigan teammate. Floyd briefed the coach on Brady's preparation, even back then, as a third-string sophomore quarterback in Ann Arbor. "As a football player, he knew everything, even then," Floyd reported. "If I had a question about a play and didn't want to go to a coach, I went to Tom because I knew he would always have the answer."

The Patriots' brain trust eventually decided it would take Brady in the third round of the draft, should he be available. Like every other player entering the draft, Brady had no idea where he'd be going and didn't know much about the Patriots, other than the fact that the team was all set at quarterback. He hoped that on Draft Day he'd get a call from his hometown team, the 49ers, a team that had failed to make the playoffs in 1999 after superstar quarterback Steve Young suffered a career-ending concussion. In Brady's boyhood dreams, the succession was clear: Montana to Young to Brady.

DRAFT DAY

Three months earlier, Brady's career at Michigan ended with his nearly flawless performance when he had thrown for 369 yards in an Orange Bowl win over Alabama. He was feeling pretty good about his chances to go relatively high in the 2000 draft. But the NFL did not invite Brady to attend the April draft held at the Theater at Madison Square Garden in New York. Those invitations were reserved for players expected to be picked early in the first round. Meanwhile, back in San Mateo, all the Bradys were gathered in the house on Portola Drive to watch the draft, televised on ESPN. The family was excited. Tommy would get drafted, not highly, but hopefully sometime during the first day. He thought he might be chosen by Mike Riley, now the second-year coach of the San Diego Chargers.

The first round of the NFL Draft is slow, lasting for hours, as each team takes the full five minutes before announcing its selection. One quarterback, Chad Pennington of Marshall University, was drafted in the opening round, No. 18 overall, by the New York Jets. Then pick after pick went by, and Tommy's name wasn't called. Eventually, as a diversion, he went off to the San Francisco Giants

The Patriots' drafting of Michigan quarterback Tom Brady would be met with little fanfare in New England.
AP PHOTO / SCOTT AUDETTE

baseball game while the family stayed home and monitored the television. Brady came back from the baseball game just before the first day ended. "He was really disappointed," said a sympathetic Nancy. "By then, my sisters and I were just watching the names on the ticker and saying, 'Okay, so who's he?' "

The second day of the draft wasn't much better, as Brady watched the proceedings on television with his family and waited for the phone to ring. It would be a long wait—a long and emotionally draining wait. Brady grew anxious as other players were being selected ahead of him. With the sixty-fifth pick in the draft, the 49ers took a quarterback from Hofstra named Giovanni Carmazzi, who would become a Rhodes Scholar but never play in an NFL regular-season game. Less than 25 miles south of San Francisco, Brady and his parents sat together in their living room watching the draft unfold on television and were stunned by the announcement. "We had season tickets for the 49ers for twenty-five years," said Brady Sr. "We were hurt. We took it personally."

Later in the third round, the Baltimore Ravens picked Chris Redman. There had now been six quarterbacks called by NFL commissioner Paul Tagliabue to elevate lowly franchises around the league as Brady continued to wait. Every time San Diego's turn came up, Brady expected a phone call. The house was silent. This was worse than what had happened at Michigan. There, Brady had discovered, he could play his way onto the field. But this was different. This wasn't about how he played. This was about how he *might* play, one day, if he ever got the chance.

"We were led to believe that he was going to be drafted, possibly second round, probably third round," Brady's father told ESPN. "They kept calling quarterback names, and we kept being stunned. With each name, it was becoming worse and worse." The third round passed. Then the fourth round came and went. About this time, Brady told his family he was going to take a walk to clear his head. He returned later to learn that another twenty-two players had been chosen, and still, his name hadn't been called.

Any hopes of hearing an NFL team announce Brady's name now appeared to be a lost cause. Most organizations are not willing to draft a quarterback in the first couple of rounds, unless they know he is a can't-miss prospect. To many, Brady was not a safe draft pick. By the fifth round, he was getting phone calls from teams asking if he would like a tryout as an undrafted free agent. This offer was the kiss of death for any football player, especially a quarterback. If a player does not get drafted, he does not usually receive any kind of signing bonus, and thus, the team does not have much of an investment in him.

Later in the fifth round, the Pittsburgh Steelers took Tennessee quarterback Tee Martin. In the sixth round, the New Orleans Saints chose West Virginia QB Marc Bulger. Then the Cleveland Browns took Spurgeon Wynn, who had completed just 47 percent of his passes at North Texas State, compared to Brady's 62 percent at Michigan. That sent Brady over the edge, and he could watch no more. "I remember him going upstairs, and he was so angry and so hurt," Nancy said.

For the first time, Brady was confronted with the potential reality that he'd have to give up his dream of playing quarterback in the NFL, and join the family business. What he didn't know was that his name was still up there on the Patriots' draft board. The idea of selecting him in the third round was quashed to address the team's more-immediate needs. Belichick wanted to boost the offense, so he picked a couple of linemen to protect Bledsoe and a running back to strengthen the ground game. In the fifth round, the Patriots selected a tight end out of Boise State named Dave Stachelski, who would play only nine games in the NFL, and none with New England.

> "Truly, the Brady story is one of the great mysteries of all time. . . . He threw four touchdown passes in the Orange Bowl against Alabama. . . . We were all asleep."
>
> —ERNIE ACCORSI, EX-NFL EXECUTIVE

As the draft chugged along, back in the Patriots offices, Rehbein and Belichick were surprised that Brady's name was still on New England's draft board. As the proceedings entered the sixth round and the Patriots were on the clock, it no longer made sense to pass on Brady. Not long after that, the phone on Portola Drive rang. It was Bill Belichick calling. The Patriots selected the kid from San Mateo in the sixth round, with the 199th pick of the draft, a pick that has since gone down as the greatest steal in NFL history. But at that moment no one knew it, no one except Dick Rehbein, who let out a celebratory yell from the team's Draft Day war room. "We got him," he exclaimed. "We got him!"

In 2011, ESPN produced a documentary, *The Brady 6*, which refers to the six quarterbacks selected before Brady in the 2000 NFL Draft. Asked in an interview about the disheartening prospect of nearly having to give up his dream of playing quarterback in the NFL, an emotional Brady cried while talking about the emotional roller-coaster ride on the day he came within fifty-five spots of not getting drafted. "I didn't want to have to be an insurance salesman, you know?"

PASSED OVER

In the sixth round, with the 199th pick of the draft, Tom Brady became a New England Patriot. It was exactly one pick sooner than the one the Green Bay Packers had used in 1959 to take a quarterback from Alabama named Bart Starr, who later would come to hire an enthusiastic young assistant named Dick Rehbein. After his name was called, a relieved Brady accepted congratulatory hugs and kisses from his family. On television, ESPN was showing highlights from his Michigan days, as draft analyst Mel Kiper Jr. offered some complimentary commentary about Brady in his analysis.

"Smart, experienced, big-game signal caller getting very high grades in the efficiency department this past season," said Kiper, who had ranked Brady as only the tenth-best quarterback in the 2000 draft. "He's a straight drop-back passer who stands tall in the pocket, doesn't show nervous feet, and does a nice job working through his progressions. He's not going to try to force the action, rarely trying to perform beyond his capability." Although Kiper added that he was impressed with Brady's play against big-time opponents in his final season, he was clearly not sold on Brady, or he wouldn't have listed him two spots behind Tim Lester, who played at Western Michigan and was not among the eleven quarterbacks drafted that year. He summed up Brady by stating: "He doesn't have the total package of skills. At the pro level, his lack of mobility could surface as a problem, and it will be interesting to see how he fares when forced to take more chances down the field."

Tom Brady developed a sense of humor about the agony of the NFL draft. As he continued to free-fall from his projected third-round draft selection, he braced himself for the real world. It's something he revealed on Facebook in 2014 when he posted his old college résumé, showing that he had years of experience as a golf course sales rep, and spent two summers interning for Merrill Lynch. His achievements and job experience were under the heading "Thomas E. Brady Jr." He graduated with a bachelor's degree in general studies in December 1999, with a GPA of 3.3 out of 4.0 from the College of Literature, Science and the Arts at the University of Michigan. At the bottom of the résumé on his Facebook page, Brady added a caption: "Found my old résumé! Really thought I was going to need this after the fifth round."

Even though he had found a way to joke about it, Brady has never forgotten the indignity of nearly getting passed over. It still motivates him. When he was told in the locker room after a playoff victory over the Baltimore Ravens following the 2014 season that he had passed Joe Montana as the all-time leader in playoff touchdown passes, he smiled and said, "That's cool. Not bad for a sixth-round pick."

WIKIMEDIA COMMONS

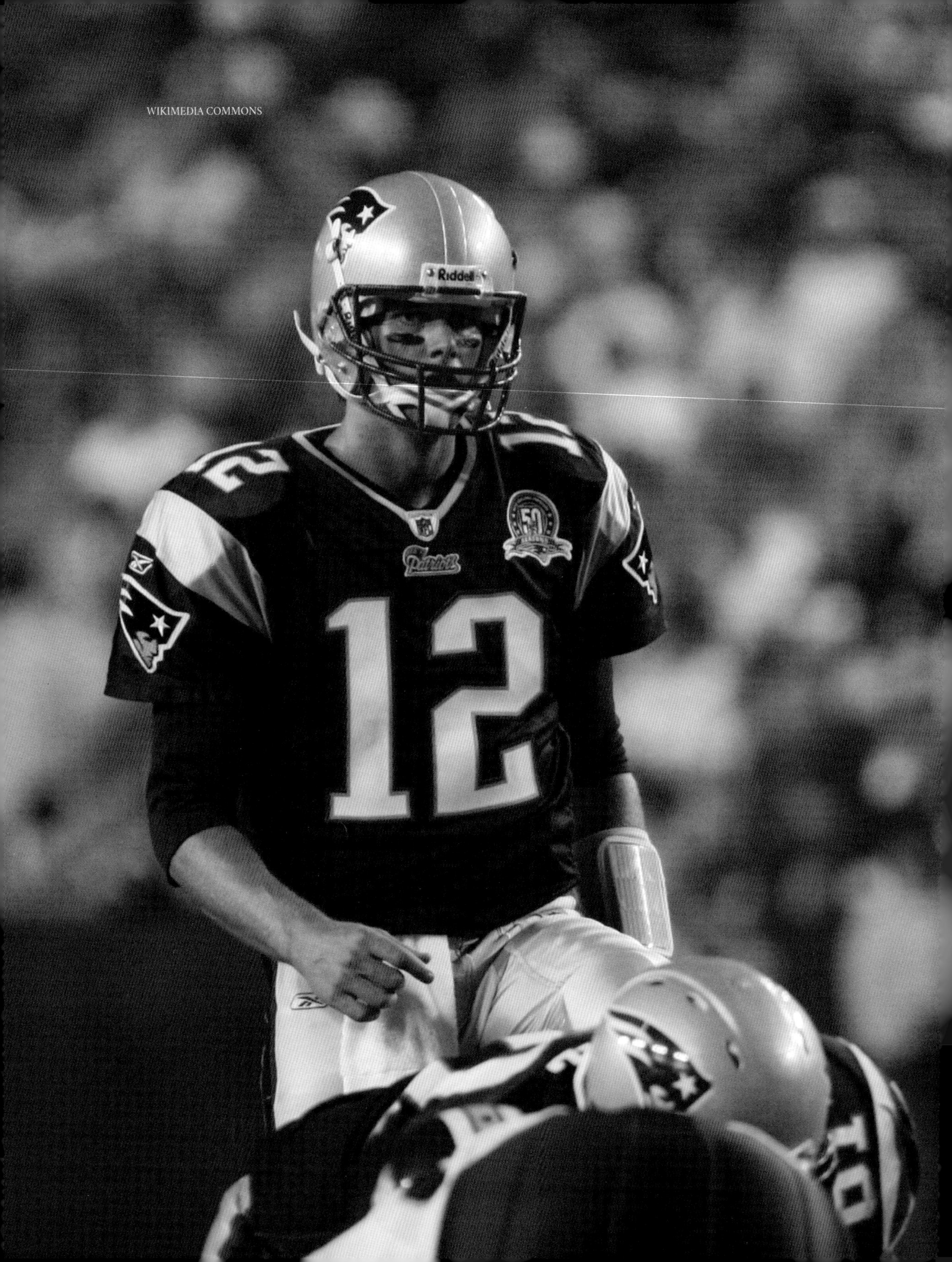

CHAPTER 5
PROVING GROUND

TOM BRADY WASN'T SELECTED UNTIL THE SIXTH ROUND OF the 2000 NFL Draft, when he was finally picked by the New England Patriots after 198 other college players, including six mostly forgotten quarterbacks, had already been chosen. "When I went in the sixth round, it wasn't anything new for me," acknowledged Brady, who had almost grown used to being overlooked. "My whole college career had been about competition. I knew I just needed to slug it out."

His selection was met in Foxborough without fanfare. He was an afterthought—a sixth-round choice—and the only buzz generated about him was by reporters covering the team who questioned why the Patriots had wasted a pick on another quarterback when they already had Drew Bledsoe, a franchise player, plus a proven veteran backup in John Friesz, and a young developmental player in Michael Bishop. "Brady Pick Hard to Figure," blared a headline in the *Boston Herald*, while an article in the *Telegram & Gazette*, a daily newspaper of Worcester, Massachusetts, called the Brady pick "somewhat curious."

Bill Belichick could ill afford a Draft Day flop heading into his first season as head coach. The moment he arrived in New England to take over the Patriots in February 2000, he realized he had inherited an underachieving team, one that was a far cry from the squad that played for coach Bill Parcells in Super Bowl XXXI, a 35–21 loss to the Green Bay Packers, in January 1997. He knew that every facet of the organization had to be improved in order to build a winner.

He also knew that Foxboro Stadium could mark the end of the line for his head coaching career if things didn't go right.

Like his coach, the unheralded rookie quarterback from Michigan also had an eye toward the future. When Patriots' owner Robert Kraft first met Brady one evening while he was leaving the team's practice facility, the quarterback was carrying a pizza box and looked more like a frat boy strolling across campus on the way to his dormitory than a legitimate NFL quarterback. Kraft noticed how lanky Brady was— "this skinny beanpole," is how the owner remembered him. The rookie walked right up to Kraft, extended his right hand, and introduced himself.

Brady told the Patriots' owner: "I'm the best decision your organization has ever made."

"Hello, Mr. Kraft. I'm Tom Brady."

"I know who you are," Kraft replied. "You're our sixth-round draft choice from Michigan."

Brady looked the billionaire owner in the eye, and with all the audacity of an undiscovered prodigy, in all seriousness, said: "I'm the best decision your organization has ever made."

The amused owner nodded and walked away, but Brady's cocksure attitude stuck with him. "It wasn't like he was arrogant, but it was more like he was very confident," said Kraft. "It was almost matter-of-fact, the way he said it. I wasn't offended at all. There was something about the way he said it, that I believed him."

"HE WAS SPECIAL"

In the spring of 2000, Brady signed his first NFL contract. He was offered the standard rookie minimum salary of $193,000 a year, but was so confident about his future that he quietly held out for a couple days before he agreed to a reported nonguaranteed three-year deal estimated at around $1 million, with a $38,500 signing bonus. He then went out and bought himself a yellow Jeep Wrangler. The twenty-two-year-old rookie settled in at the Endzone Motor Inn, a few miles

Tom Brady knew his rookie season in the NFL was essentially going to be a redshirt year.
AP PHOTO / STEPHAN SAVOIA

south of Foxboro Stadium, where the Patriots lodged their rookies and fringe free agents for the summer.

When he arrived at his first training camp, as a late-round pick on a team with four quarterbacks, Brady was the furthest thing from a lock to make the Patriots' roster. His position was similar to the one he had faced at Michigan. He was at the bottom rung of a ladder and hadn't been given any assurances about reaching the next rung, let alone moving all the way to the top one. What's more, this was the NFL, and Bill Belichick, New England's demanding head coach, hadn't given him a four-year scholarship. If Brady didn't make a positive impression

SECRET SKILL

The best way for a rookie to ingratiate himself with the organization is by being a great player on the field and a great person off the field. But the best way for a rookie to ingratiate himself within the locker room is by going out with the guys. Brady quickly became one of the guys during his rookie year and impressed the linemen with his ability to drink beer and show no effect. Brady's beer drinking from his younger days in the NFL is still legendary. "No one on the team could beat him chugging a beer," said linebacker Tedy Bruschi. "Linemen couldn't beat the kid. I remember seeing it for the first time and thinking, *Holy smokes, are you serious?* He was crushing guys."

Everyone marveled with the impressive speed at which Brady chugged a beer. "You couldn't have poured out the beer faster into a glass," remembered Brian Hoyer, describing Brady's secret skill, witnessed at a team dinner, after much convincing, when Brady took part in a beer-chugging contest. Brady drained his glass faster than any of the linemen. "It was unbelievable," Hoyer added. "And he slams the mug on the table and puts both fists in the air. He walks away with a look on his face that said, 'You really thought you were going to beat me on this?' The place went nuts."

Brady rarely reveals his elite beer-drinking skills, breaking out his concealed talent only from time to time. The most prominent example was on an episode of *The Late Show* with Stephen Colbert, in March 2018. Brady was promoting his book *The TB12 Method*, in which he writes about diet and athletic performance. That includes abstaining from alcohol. Brady told Colbert he rarely drinks beer, but acknowledged that he was a "pretty good beer chugger back in the day." So the host challenged him to a contest. Brady drained his glass within seconds after two gulps, with Colbert finishing a distant last.

quickly, Belichick would have no reservations about releasing him and searching for another fourth-string quarterback.

Brady was playing behind three other signal-callers, and although he wasn't given much chance of rising higher, or getting any playing time, he focused his attention on every detail of his responsibilities. He studied Coach Belichick's playbook so thoroughly that he could recite all of the plays. Brady came well prepared to the team's pre-camp quarterback school. He was the only rookie, but he projected the calm demeanor of a student who knows he's ready for a big exam.

"The rest of us waited for him to start asking rookie questions, like every rookie does when he comes into the NFL," said backup QB John Friesz, a ten-year veteran. "There are things you just don't know as a rookie. Not Tom. He didn't ask a single rookie question. I was scratching my head at how advanced he was before he even stepped on the practice field. I knew right then he was special."

Although Brady did not get many reps during practice, he did show poise when he got the chance to run the offense. He corrected the receivers when they ran the wrong route or when another player made a mistake. He could monitor the entire offense. Almost immediately, Brady caught the eye of Charlie Weis, New England's offensive coordinator. He tirelessly trained with Weis and quarterbacks coach Dick Rehbein, refining the techniques that Tom Martinez had taught him years before.

Brady was constantly watching the veteran players and taking mental notes on how they played. And even then, he displayed a level of leadership

"He's the ultimate franchise quarterback. He does everything right."
—RON WOLF, HALL OF FAME EXECUTIVE

that impressed his veteran teammates. When he thought he saw a better way for something to be done, he spoke up and offered his advice. But he also knew when to pick his spots and when to remain quiet. "He's quick and observant," said punter Ken Walter. "But he also knows when not to talk, and that's just as important."

Brady was smart enough to become friends with his offensive linemen. Even as he fought for a roster spot, he risked Belichick's wrath in practices by trying to protect his teammates, particularly the linemen who blocked for him. "There were times," center Grey Ruegamer recalled, "when I would screw up and Belichick started riding my butt, and Tom would say, 'Hey, Coach, that was on me, not him.' He would take a bullet for a teammate. That kind of loyalty goes a long way."

Tom Brady was getting a taste of life as a rookie in the NFL—on and off the field. During an initiation rite, Bledsoe put confetti in the air-conditioning vents of Brady's yellow Jeep, and turned the fan on high. When Brady put the key in the ignition and started his car, the inside of the vehicle suddenly looked like Times Square on New Year's Eve. Naturally, Bledsoe was sitting in his car next to Brady's, enjoying the show.

MAKING THE GRADE

In the late summer of 2000, Brady drew on his signing bonus for a down payment on a spacious condominium in Franklin, Massachusetts, conveniently located just ten minutes from the team's practice facility. It's not unusual for a professional athlete to buy a condo near his team's practice facility. But in the NFL, where rookie contracts are not guaranteed, most players in Brady's position live as renters until they are more established in the league and have the financial security of a long-term contract or a lucrative signing bonus. Brady's decision to buy a home as a sixth-round pick on a roster of four quarterbacks was tangible evidence that his famous declaration to owner Robert Kraft wasn't just bluster. Brady believed it, and was willing to make a financial investment in his future.

Wisely, he took on rent-paying rookie roommates for the three-bedroom spread, enlisting defensive tackle David Nugent from Purdue University, taken two picks after Brady, at number 201, and tight end Chris Eitzmann, an undrafted free agent from Harvard University, to help make ends meet. Eitzmann performed extra chores for his young quarterback (and landlord) by staying after practice a minimum of thirty minutes to run routes so Brady could practice his throwing accuracy. "Brady just wanted to keep going and going and going," said Eitzmann. "He'd have me run the entire tight-end route package. We would just run them until I was dead."

Early in training camp, an indomitable work ethic was the first thing the New England Patriots and their coaches saw in their sixth-round draft choice as he directed the scout team, which is made up of rookies and undistinguished

Coach Bill Belichick saw something special in Tom Brady, and rewarded the rookie quarterback with a coveted spot on the Patriots' fifty-three-man roster. AP PHOTO / VICTORIA AROCHO

players from the practice squad. The scout team's job is to simulate the offense of the upcoming opponent. However, after practice, Brady and the scout team would run through the New England offense. Watching Brady with the rookies, coaches noticed that he was making them better. He stood out as a leader, and the players matured around him. "They'd go through the plays, and, if somebody got something wrong, he'd correct them," recalled Belichick. "You could see them getting better and better. They moved on you."

Backup QB John Friesz had never seen a quarterback so tirelessly analyze film of himself leading a scout team in practice. He was also impressed by the way Brady had taken what he had been given—a group of fellow rookies and other players who hadn't been around long enough to be considered castoffs—and out of it he was creating a team around him. Brady led, and the other players followed him.

Although he was making a positive impression, upon initial inspection, some veteran Patriots weren't sure what to make of the rookie quarterback.

Linebacker Willie McGinest said he thought Brady "needed to get his ass in the weight room and get in shape. We were all joking with him and messing with him about his combine tape." Running back J. R. Redmond said he remembered the quarterback "being about the worst athlete you could ever put in an NFL uniform." They also saw early signs of Brady becoming a Belichick disciple. The coach, stern as ever in his first full team meeting, recited his litany of rules, then surprised the rookies with an oral quiz.

"Brady," he barked at the rookie quarterback. "What do you tell the media if you tear a knee ligament and they ask you about the injury?"

"You say you have a bad leg," Brady replied, parroting Belichick's instructions to say as little as possible.

The coach soon began to recognize Brady's special traits, among them his obsessive preparation. Belichick raved about the quarterback's relentless film study, his almost instant mastery of the playbook, and his commitment to working with scout-team receivers late at night. He also was impressed with Brady's football IQ, and continually challenged the rookie to adapt to the pro-style game. The coach spent each practice working against Brady, testing him, disrupting his pre-snap reads and passes. He would pour water onto the football just before the snap to make it difficult for the center and Brady to handle. The defense would be told the coming offensive play call in order to jump the receivers' route or quickly fill the hole to meet the running back.

Everything during these early practices was set up to make life hard on the ascending young quarterback and the offensive group he was charged with leading. After one especially rough practice, Belichick laid into Brady with a vicious tongue-lashing. It wasn't that Brady was playing poorly or misreading his keys; the offense had merely stalled out because the defense was given the game plan ahead of time and could predict Brady's every move.

Linebacker Matt Chatham approached Brady in the lunchroom after practice. "I said that we were being encouraged to jump certain routes, grab and hold, and make life unusually difficult for him," Chatham recalled. The linebacker told Brady that he would be happy to back off so that the quarterback could find his rhythm again.

"No way," Brady replied angrily. "Keep it coming. We need it."

To Brady, practice does not make perfect. Perfect practice makes perfect.

"I love seeing us get better," he said, "and I don't think you get better in games. The improvements come in practice."

The mark of Brady's leadership is that he infuses practice time with a competitive atmosphere and challenges teammates by simulating game-time conditions during training sessions. What does Brady do when a practice-squad player intercepts him? He rewards that player. Former teammate Donté Stallworth has tweeted about Brady's motivational techniques. "Brady actually paid practice squad [players] if they picked him off in practice," the wide receiver wrote in October 2015.

After playing well in two preseason games, Belichick rewarded the rookie quarterback with a precious spot on the fifty-three-man roster. "We'll just run him out there and see what happens," said the coach. The decision to keep Brady took many by surprise. After all, in making the announcement, Belichick said he had no immediate plans for the kid, and admitted that carrying four quarterbacks meant the Patriots were sacrificing a roster spot to keep Brady on the

team—even though he would not play much, if at all. But Belichick was making a statement. "Bill definitely saw something in him," said guard Joe Andruzzi. "You never hear of teams keeping a fourth-string quarterback."

Brady showed early signs of becoming a Belichick disciple.

The Patriots' equipment manager issued Brady a uniform with the number 12, a jersey number that held no particular significance for the franchise. It was a number that had been given to past quarterbacks such as backup Matt Cavanaugh, and even to a punter. No Patriot had worn the number 12 with distinction, but the rookie quarterback was determined to change that.

"THIS AIN'T CLUB MED"

Coach Bill Belichick had low expectations for the 2000 season. In his opinion the players on his team simply weren't tough enough. "We've got too many people who are overweight, too many guys who are out of shape, and too many guys who haven't paid the price they need to pay at this time of the year. You can't win with forty good players while the other team has fifty-three," he groused during training camp.

Belichick was intent on finding his kind of players, and weeding out those who wouldn't commit to his brand of smart, tough, and emotionally challenging professional football. "This ain't Club Med" was a constant reminder that the coaching staff used to chide the players. The Patriots were known to practice longer, with far more physical practices, than was the NFL norm of the time.

Belichick's pessimistic outlook for the 2000 Patriots proved prescient, and at the outset, the regular season was a struggle. The team stumbled out of the gate, dropping their first four games. Belichick didn't notch his first victory as New England's head coach until Week 5, when his team beat the Broncos 28–19 in Denver. After winning two games in a row, the Patriots lost their next four in increasingly ugly fashion. In Week 11, they traveled to Cleveland, site of Belichick's unremarkable first head-coaching position, where he was greeted by boos and a sign reading: "You Still Stink." Bledsoe, hampered by a sore right thumb, threw an interception and lost three fumbles in a dreadful 19–11 loss.

Although Bledsoe had struggled since the second half of the 1999 season, he wasn't truly in jeopardy of losing his job to Brady—at least, not yet— because back then, Brady was still on the margins, the last quarterback on the bottom of the totem pole. He spent almost every game day on the sidelines. In fact, he was inactive for the first nine games on the schedule, meaning that he did not even dress in uniform for the games. Brady was so seldom required to do anything on game day that, as a rookie, he idly scarfed junk food before kickoffs while his teammates prepared for action.

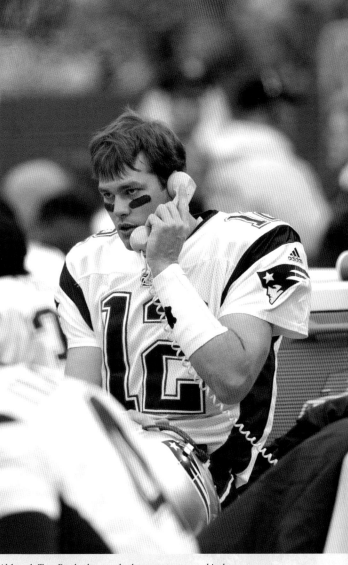

Although Tom Brady threw only three passes as a rookie, he prepared for each game as if he was going to be the starting quarterback. MITCHELL B. REIBEL VIA AP

"I got to eat nachos before the game," he recalled. "I didn't know if I was dressing or active. I just had to bring my playbook to the meetings. That was as much as I had to do that year."

Brady's parents went to games anyway, arriving three hours early so they could watch their son throw in warm-ups. Before a game at Foxboro Stadium against the San Diego Chargers (in 2001), a woman introduced herself to

Galynn and Tom Sr., and said, "My husband just loves your son." The woman turned out to be Dallas Pioli, wife of Patriots' general manager Scott Pioli, and Bill Parcells's daughter. She told them how much her husband raved about Brady being the first one in the building and the last one to leave—and then, according to her husband, "he comes back again at 11:30 at night when no one is around." Scott Pioli had been getting phone calls from security guards at the stadium that the kid was trying to get into the building to do extra work in the dead of night. Pioli drove over to check, and there was Brady's car, that distinctive yellow Jeep Wrangler, in the parking lot at one o'clock in the morning.

> "He's a heck of a player, and he's such a competitor. What's been most impressive to me is his fire and spirit."
> —BRETT FAVRE, HALL OF FAME QB

Despite his remarkable dedication, Brady remained a practice player. This meant that he rarely traveled for away games. One of his roommates, David Nugent, recalled returning home from road games early in the morning when Brady didn't travel with the team and finding him hunched over a coffee table, studying his playbook. "I said, 'Tom, how do you not get frustrated?' " Nugent recalled. "He said, 'I can't control what anybody else thinks of me. All I can do is focus on the things I *can* control, like how much I know the playbook, how hard I practice, and how hard I work out.' "

"FRUSTRATING SEASON"

Each week, Brady prepared as if he would be the starting quarterback for the upcoming game. He wanted to be ready. For several hours each week, he routinely watched tapes of the opposition. He wanted to be familiar with their tactics, weaknesses, and strengths. On the field, a quarterback has to make split-second decisions. He wanted to be able to anticipate what a defense might do on a particular play. From the sidelines, he critiqued Bledsoe's game and kept a mental log of what he did and did not do well. When Bledsoe was bothered by a thumb injury, Brady got more practice reps with the starters, going against multiple

As a rookie, Tom Brady displayed an ability to ingratiate himself in the locker room, and quickly became one of the guys. AP PHOTO / CARLOS OSORIO

defenses and facing an assortment of blitzes. Gradually, he became more comfortable leading the other starting players.

The rookie quarterback finally dressed in uniform for a game in Week 11, but only because Belichick ignored the noise emanating from Patriots fans. With Bledsoe listed as questionable because of an injury, the Patriots website polled fans on which backup quarterback they favored. The landslide winner was Bishop, with 78.5 percent of the vote, followed by Friesz (12.8 percent), and Brady (8.7 percent). Bledsoe managed to start the game, a 16–13 win over Cincinnati, but Belichick, bucking the fans, had elevated Brady above Bishop that week on the depth chart.

Eleven days later, on Thanksgiving Day, Brady made his NFL debut in Detroit, calling four plays in the fourth quarter of a 34–9 defeat, the team's worst spanking of the season. In his professional return to the state of Michigan, Brady completed 1 out of 3 passes for a total of 6 yards. The first one he threw was very nearly intercepted and returned for a touchdown, a step up from the first pass he'd thrown at Michigan, which actually was. The loss dropped the Patriots to 3-9, and Brady was stunned afterward that many of his teammates appeared indifferent. "Why does it seem like nobody really cares?" Friesz recalled Brady complaining. Friesz explained that the team had lost its shot at the playoffs, and that professional football players often react differently to wins and losses than collegians. "None of it made sense to him," Friesz said. "He didn't like the quit he saw."

Brady got into that one Thanksgiving Day game, but did not play again his rookie season. For the Patriots, the year ended as miserably as it began, losing to the Miami Dolphins, 27–24, on a long field goal with nine seconds remaining in the fourth quarter. After the loss, Bledsoe—who was sacked 45 times that year, tied for fourth-most in the league—sounded exhausted. "It was the most frustrating season of my career," he told reporters. "I'm worn out mentally, physically, and emotionally." New England finished the season at 5-11, dead last in their division, the AFC East. The Patriots offense would score 30 points only once that season, during a meaningless December victory against the Kansas City Chiefs. Bledsoe quarterbacked the seventh-worst-scoring team in the league. There were rumblings that Coach Belichick's job might be on the line if major improvement was not forthcoming. The offense needed a massive jolt. From where it would come was still a mystery.

Brady knew the 2000 season was essentially going to be a redshirt year for him. He correctly anticipated hardly any playing time, but he was determined to take the long view of his career. Even after his agonizing humiliation in the NFL draft left him as a fourth-string rookie reserve for the Patriots, Brady kept trying to tell people back home he was going to make it. He watched the Patriots' starter, Drew Bledsoe, and told his high school teammate, wide receiver John Kirby, and his best friend, Kevin Krystofiak: "Guys, I can play with this guy. I do a lot of things better than him." They likely didn't believe him—and for good reason, since once the season started the rookie quarterback was firmly glued to the bench. But Brady's confidence was unwavering. After the season, at a buddy's wedding, he told Aaron Shea, the former Michigan tight end, that he was going to beat out Bledsoe for the starting job. "Dude," Shea said, "this is Drew Bledsoe we're talking about."

To Brady, it didn't matter if his competition was named Drew Henson or Drew Bledsoe. All that mattered was getting the chance to prove he could play.

CHAPTER 6
CHAMPIONSHIP METTLE

DURING HIS ROOKIE SEASON OF 2000, TOM BRADY HAD SPENT almost every game day on the sidelines. In fact, he was inactive for all but two of the team's games, and wound up throwing only three passes in the one game in which he did receive a few minutes of playing time. It was a situation that Brady had no argument with. "When I got here, I was so far from being an NFL quarterback," acknowledged Brady. "I wasn't strong enough or quick enough to play at that level."

Bill Belichick told Brady that the only way he would stick with the Patriots past the first season would be for him to get quicker and stronger, and to improve his passing mechanics. Brady heard the message loud and clear. He worked diligently during his first season to bulk up physically and to improve his strength and technique. In the off-season, Brady participated in every one of the team's sixty workouts, even though most of them weren't mandatory.

By the time the team had reassembled in July to begin training for the 2001 season, Brady had added 15 pounds of muscle, which helped him to increase his arm strength. And while he still wasn't a fast runner, he now was also able to out-run teammates he hadn't been able to keep up with a year earlier. As his legs got stronger, he could take a hit better. He could stand in the pocket and complete passes even while he was being tackled.

After an injury sidelined Drew Bledsoe, left, Tom Brady became the Patriots' starting quarterback and kept the job for nearly two decades. AP PHOTO / AL MESSERSCHMIDT

"At training camp you could see how much work he had put in during the off-season," said center Damien Woody. "His throwing mechanics were much smoother and, as practices went on, we started to get a good idea of what he might be capable of." Belichick was even more enthusiastic than Woody. "I'm not sure I've ever seen any player improve as much as Tom has in such a short time," said the coach. "When he came to training camp, right away, everybody saw the dramatic improvement." The rest of the coaching staff also noted the big differ-ence, and they saw the results translated onto the field in Brady's performances during training camp and in preseason games. Daily, Brady strove to be the best player on the field. The Pats' offensive coordinator Charlie Weis noticed Brady's solid play and saw how he worked harder than anyone else in the weight room.

Things were looking up for Brady in his second season. John Friesz had called it a career, putting Brady in line to compete with Michael Bishop to become the team's backup quarterback. But prior to the season, the Patriots had brought in veteran QB Damon Huard, who had won five of six starts in Miami, to back up Bledsoe. The situation resonated with Brady. He'd been through all of this at Michigan. A chance would open up, and then it would close.

> "We saw things that made us decide to make Tom [Brady] the No. 2. He showed us that he might turn out to be special."
>
> —CHARLIE WEIS, EX-PATRIOTS COACH

CRUNCH TIME

The second pro football training camp of his career proved pivotal for Brady. Inactive for 14 games in 2000, he had returned for his second year bigger and stronger, and a little bit faster, though his running style still evoked a panting stockbroker chasing after a bus. Desperate to learn the offense's intricacies and improve his throwing delivery, Brady worked tirelessly with quarterbacks coach Dick Rehbein. The two football fanatics forged a tight bond, with Rehbein, forty-five, serving as the de facto older brother that Brady never had. Sadly, during training camp at Bryant College in August, Rehbein died unexpectedly of a heart attack. With the season-opener approaching, Belichick took over Rehbein's duties, meaning, he had to work with Brady.

Apparently, Belichick was impressed. Brady was so sharp in the preseason, he jumped ahead of Bishop, who was waived and went off to NFL Europe. The veteran Huard had a good camp, but Brady had a better one. As a result, on the eve of the '01 season, Belichick announced that Brady, not Huard, would back up Bledsoe. "It was a big decision, but it wasn't a hard decision," Belichick said the day he promoted Brady to second string. "Tom has a lot of natural leadership."

With his rapid development, Brady started the season on the bench, as the second banana behind Bledsoe, where he might have remained for the rest of the season

THE COMEBACK KID

We've seen Tom Brady orchestrate numerous comebacks throughout his NFL career. In fact, including postseason play, he's engineered an NFL record—62 game-winning performances—to lead his team to a victory from a fourth-quarter deficit or tie (through the 2020 season), six more than Peyton Manning. On October 14, 2001, fans got to experience the first.

New England was down 19–16 early in the fourth quarter against the Chargers, and poor old San Diego thought it had it made in the shade when the team went up 26–16, with 8:48 left in the game. But if there's one thing we know by now, Tom Brady doesn't care about time. No. 12 trotted onto the field, his Patriots facing a 10-point deficit and an uphill climb, and proceeded to spark a thrilling 29–26 overtime win.

The twenty-four-year-old Californian showed poise, confidence, and complete control while engineering the Pats to a field goal, touchdown, and field goal over the final three drives. The next day's headline from the *Boston Globe* read: "Understudy Steals Show." The remarkable events that had transpired, elapsing in about one hour in real time, flipped the trajectory of the Patriots' season, and sparked Brady's legendary career.

"He put himself on the map today," backup Patriots QB Damon Huard said. "He was calm, cool, and collected."

"Never a doubt, huh?" Brady said, opening his postgame press conference. "Never a doubt."

And just like that, a legend began to take form.

had not fate intervened. For in the team's second game, Bledsoe suffered a serious injury when New York Jets linebacker Mo Lewis leveled him with a sickening hit. "I still remember the way it sounded; it was like two cars crashing," said Brady. "It was two huge bodies running at full speed and Drew just got massacred."

The blow sheared an artery in Bledsoe's chest, forcing him to leave the game and give way to Brady. But the understudy wasn't able to jump-start the Pats' offense, which managed to score just 3 points, and New England still hadn't won a game all season. The Patriots finally stood on the winning sideline the following week, with Brady making his first NFL start, a 44–13 wipeout of the division rival Indianapolis Colts before 60,292 curious fans at Foxboro Stadium. Peyton Manning, the twenty-five-year-old Pro Bowl quarterback, got snookered into throwing 3 interceptions and taking 2 sacks. Although Brady didn't play a key role in the victory in terms of productivity—he threw for just 168 yards, with no touchdowns or interceptions—he didn't make any mistakes, either. Afterward, he signed a game ball and delivered it to Tom Martinez as a symbol of gratitude from a pupil to his former tutor.

The Patriots' poor start to the 2001 season left many New Englanders no choice but to count the days until the Red Sox and Nomar Garciaparra reported to spring training.
AP PHOTO / CHARLES KRUPA

Instead of building on success, Brady took the team to Miami and, making his second NFL start, played one of his worst games as a pro. He went 12-for-24 for 87 yards and was sacked 4 times in a 30–10 drubbing by the Dolphins. Most embarrassing, he dropped a snap on the final play of the third quarter, and after guard Grey Ruegamer inadvertently kicked the ball, Miami's Jason Taylor scooped it up and scored. "That's just 1 play of 20 plays that should have been a lot better than we executed," Brady said.

After 4 games in 2001, the Patriots' record stood at 1-3. The season seemed to be slipping toward mediocrity, if not total disaster. Despite all the great press notices he'd received in training camp, Brady had looked ordinary in his first two starts. New England fans who hadn't already given up on the season anxiously

Holy Tuck! Tom Brady's fumble was ruled an incomplete pass, handing New England a big break in a playoff game against the Oakland Raiders.
AP PHOTO / ELISE AMENDOLA

listened for news about Bledsoe's return, while those fans who *had* given the team up for dead were left to count the days until the Boston Celtics tipped off the NBA season, and the Red Sox reported to spring training.

Their prospects seemed to dim still further when San Diego's head coach, Mike Riley (a Brady fan from way back), brought his Chargers into Foxboro Stadium the following week and rocked New England back on its heels. The Chargers waltzed to a 26–16 lead with time getting tight in the fourth quarter, and the visitors were already starting to think about an enjoyable flight to the West Coast. But Brady suddenly started to click, connecting on 13 of his final 19 passes, and marching the Patriots offense down the field on three consecutive scoring drives. "Brady played the game of his life," said Chargers linebacker Junior Seau. "We couldn't get them off the field."

Brady's comeback win in overtime against San Diego was the game when everything changed.

Brady had a huge day, going 33-of-54 for 364 yards and 2 touchdowns in New England's 29–26 comeback win, in overtime. "Tom played with a lot of poise," Belichick said of the second-year pro, who was now 2-1 as a starter in place of an injured Bledsoe. "We really fought our way out of a tough situation," said Brady, who was named AFC Player of the Week in only his third NFL start. "That's the type of stuff you really build on as a team."

Tom Brady, who was playing in just the fifth game of his NFL career, found his late-game touch and rallied the Patriots from a formidable 10-point deficit and helped set up Adam Vinatieri's 44-yard field goal in overtime to lead the Patriots to a breathless victory. "That was the game," Charlie Weis said, "when everything changed."

THE BIG STAGE

Brady had put himself on the map by directing such an improbable comeback victory as a quarterback so young in years and NFL experience. The way he responded late in the game and during overtime had left an indelible impression on Bill Belichick, who was generous in his assessment of Brady's performance. "His decision-making is a real strength," said the coach. "He understands coverages and where the openings are going to be." By degrees, the Patriots were becoming Tom Brady's team.

He sparkled once again the following week in the Pats' second meeting of the season against the Colts, completing 80 percent of his attempts and throwing a trio of TD passes in New England's 38–17 win at Indianapolis. But he followed that dream game with a nightmarish one against the Broncos. The Pats not only lost the game, but Brady, who had so far thrown 162 passes without an interception, was picked off four times in Denver. His teammates and coaches knew that a performance like that had the potential to send a player, especially a young, untested quarterback, into mental paralysis. Brady erased those doubts by bouncing right back and throwing 3 touchdown passes with no interceptions in the team's next game, a 24–10 win over the Atlanta Falcons.

"I've had hard times before," said Brady, who refuses to allow a bad performance to knock him off his stride. "You learn how to deal with them and just move forward. You have to know how to put everything behind you, because you can't get last week back." It's that mental toughness, as much as Brady's quarterbacking skills, which convinced Belichick to stick with him as the team's starter, even after Bledsoe had fully recovered from his injury.

"Tom's the starter," the coach said. "That's the way it's going to be. I think it's pretty clear-cut."

Brady went on to reward his coach's decision by leading the Patriots on a roll. New England won 6 straight games to finish the season with a flourish, an 11-5 record, and possession of the AFC East title for the first time in the Brady-Belichick era. "I think at some point you have to sit back and evaluate and say, 'Wow, this has been a pretty good year,'" said Brady, in what qualifies as a pretty good understatement. "I don't think it's as much about how far I've come, but about how far we've come as an offense."

In his first season as a starter, Brady didn't merely stand in; he stood out, throwing for 2,843 yards and completing 63.9 percent of his passes. He had begun the season as an understudy, and finished it by being named to the Pro Bowl: at the time, only the fifth quarterback in NFL history to earn the honor in the season of his first start. Tom Brady had come a long way. "If you look at everything he's been through, Tom has defeated all the odds," his high school teammate, Steven Loerke, told the *St. Louis Post-Dispatch*. "If there was one word I'd use to describe him, it would be *perseverance*."

Tom Brady needed all the resolve he could muster just to arrive in time for the start of his first playoff game, which was played against the Oakland Raiders on a night in which winds swirled and steadily falling snow covered the turf at Foxboro Stadium. The wintry conditions threw a wet blanket over the teams' offenses, and at halftime Brady had completed only 6 passes for 74 yards, and the Pats trailed, 7–0. Instead of slinking off to a corner of the locker room, however, Brady collected the offense around him and let them know that the second half would be different. "He gathered the squad and told them that they could do better, and that he would do better," said Pats' safety Lawyer Milloy. "He's young, but he's a leader."

In the second half, Brady backed up his brave locker-room words by passing for 238 yards and scrambling into the end zone for a touchdown that cut the deficit to 13–10, with less than eight minutes to play. But he really showed his colors near the end of the fourth quarter, with the weather worsening by the moment, when he directed an 8-play drive that set up Adam Vinatieri's game-tying 45-yard field goal with only twenty-seven seconds left in regulation. The crucial play of the drive was not without controversy.

The Raiders were still leading by 3 points with under two minutes left when Brady, operating out of the shotgun, dropped back to pass. Oakland cornerback Charles Woodson, who'd played with Brady at Michigan, came through untouched on a blitz and clobbered Brady. The ball popped away, and linebacker Greg Biekert fell on it at the Oakland 42 with 1:47 left, apparently salting the

Tom Brady couldn't avoid the rush of being named the most valuable player of the Patriots' 20–17 win over the Rams in Super Bowl XXXVI. AP PHOTO / STEPHAN SAVOIA

game away for the Raiders. The Patriots were out of time-outs. Oakland merely had to kneel down three times and the game would be over.

The Patriots appealed the play, and the referee ducked under the awning to watch it again on video review. It seemed that Brady had been bringing his arm forward, and that he had not "tucked" it back against his body. It didn't matter how much it looked like a fumble. Under the rules it was determined that Brady had thrown an incomplete pass. The referee reversed the ruling on the field, and New England got the ball back. Four plays later, Vinatieri made the game-tying kick through the blizzard in four inches of snow. Under the circumstances, it might've been the most improbable kick in NFL history.

Of course, the Raiders stood no chance in overtime. The Patriots won the coin toss, and with the snow still falling and darkness descending around the flood-lit stadium, Brady completed 8 straight passes to move the ball down to the Raiders 5-yard line, perfectly positioning Vinatieri's 23-yard game-winning 3-pointer. "He never seems to get rattled," said wide receiver Troy Brown, one of the team's veterans. "You never see him put his head down or get upset about making a bad throw. The way he behaves lets people know that he has confidence in what he's doing, and that, in turn, makes us believe that we can get it done."

Belichick, who had watched and suffered as the Patriots staggered through a 5-11 finish the year before, appreciated just how far the team had come in one season. "I can't say enough about this group," he said. "They will not quit. To pull our way back we had to make a lot of big plays. It can't get much closer than it did." The quarterback had already earned a Pro Bowl appearance in his first season as a starter, and now he stood one win away from the Super Bowl. Of his overturned fumble, soon to be known as the infamous "Tuck Rule" play, Brady said, with a sheepish grin, "I was throwing the ball, definitely. And even if I wasn't, that's my story and I'm sticking to it."

After Brady went down with a sprained left ankle in the first half of the AFC Championship Game, Bledsoe rode to the rescue by directing the team to a 24–17 upset of the Pittsburgh Steelers, who had compiled a conference-best 13-3 record. Because of that unlikely escape, some termed New England a team of destiny, but that ignores the hard work that made this triumph possible. Yet after watching Brady move effectively during practice in the days before the Super Bowl, Belichick did not hesitate in naming him the starter. "I sure hope there are bigger days ahead in bigger arenas," Brady said.

There would be. And Brady would be the headliner.

FROM LAST TO FIRST

The Patriots and their young quarterback arrived in New Orleans for Super Bowl XXXVI to face off against a St. Louis Rams team that had posted an NFL-best 14-2 record, which included a 24–17 win over the Pats in Week 10. The Rams had a potent offense—known as The Greatest Show on Turf—which featured most of the same players who had led St. Louis to a Super Bowl victory two years earlier, including a pair of future Hall of Famers in quarterback Kurt Warner and running back Marshall Faulk.

Belichick's decision to put the ball back in No. 12's hands for the Super Bowl showdown, and to tie the team's fortunes to its first-year starter, was not met with much surprise. If ever a coach had his finger on the pulse of a team, it was the forty-nine-year-old Belichick, whose firm but fair style helped guide the Pats from last place in 2000 to first place in '01. "It's really a dream come true to be a quarterback and start a Super Bowl game," said Brady, his eyes twinkling. "It's probably the highlight of my life, so far."

Because this was the first Super Bowl after the September 11 terrorist attacks, there was a patriotic theme leading up to the game in New Orleans. The pregame festivities featured songs and other events honoring America and those who were lost in the attacks. For- mer president George H. W. Bush participated in the coin toss with Hall of Famer Roger Staubach, who had won the Heisman Trophy as a member of the US Naval Academy. The Patriots set the tone early by changing the Super Bowl pregame introductions forever. Instead of being introduced as individuals, the Patriots elected to take the field as a team. "It represented what we were," said Larry Izzo. "There were no stars on that team."

Belichick was playing to avoid overtime; he trusted Brady not to make a mistake.

The Patriots may have been the underdogs when they ran onto the Louisiana Superdome field, but after Brady threw a short touchdown pass to wide receiver David Patten on an out-and-up route near the end of the second quarter, it was the New Englanders who went into the locker room with a 14–3 halftime lead. Brady had helped free his receiver with a pump fake that froze Rams' cornerback Dexter McCleon for a split second—all the time that an NFL receiver needs to separate himself from his defender—and Patten made a tumbling catch in the back of the end zone. "A huge throw, because we didn't want to settle for a field goal there," said Patten of Brady's strike. "He put the ball right where it had to be."

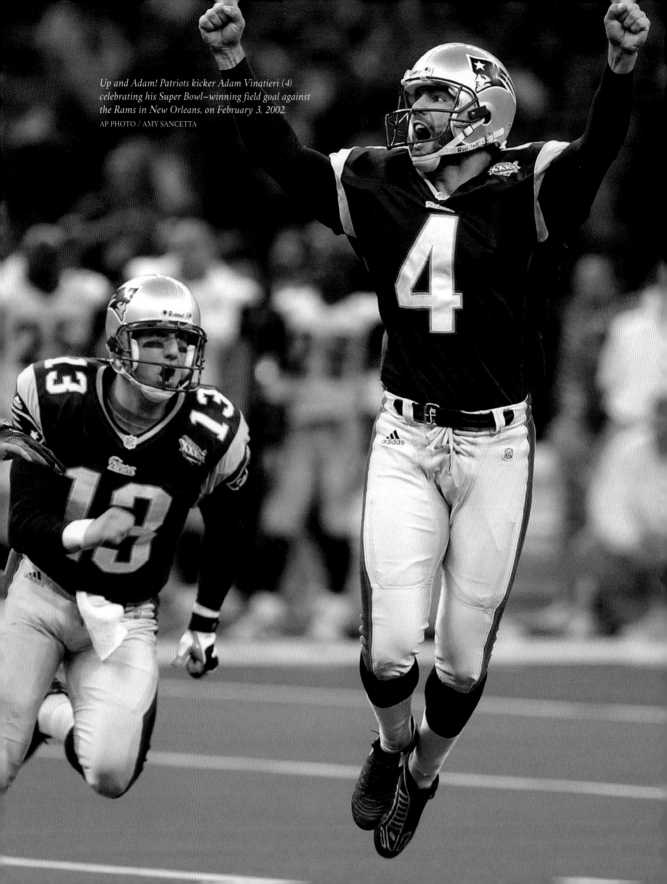

Up and Adam! Patriots kicker Adam Vinatieri (4) celebrating his Super Bowl–winning field goal against the Rams in New Orleans, on February 3, 2002.
AP PHOTO / AMY SANCETTA

Brady, however, struggled to complete passes in the second half, and the Pats' offense stalled. Meanwhile, the Rams came back to tie the score at 17, with 90 seconds left in regulation time, setting up Brady's first of many star turns. The Patriots took over on their own 17-yard line with 1:21 remaining. The smart play was to let the clock run and take a chance on winning in overtime. In fact, up in the Fox Television booth, the sport's most prominent analyst, John Madden—a respected Super Bowl–winning coach with the Oakland Raiders, who was influential enough to create his own video-game dynasty, *Madden NFL*—famously told the 86.8 million people watching that Belichick, with no time-outs and poor field position, should run out the clock and play for overtime. "I don't think you want to force anything here," Madden said. "You don't want to do anything stupid, because you have no time-outs and you're backed up." Actually, Belichick was playing to *avoid* overtime.

"WE ARE ALL PATRIOTS"

The Patriots took possession of the football on their own 17-yard line with 1:21 remaining in Super Bowl XXXVI and the score tied, 17–17. Brady, Belichick, and the offensive coordinator, Charlie Weis, huddled on the sideline. Belichick was now facing a question that would shape the rest of his career. Should he go for the win and trust that his young quarterback wouldn't commit a fatal turnover, or should he run out the clock and take his chances in overtime? "It was a ten-second conversation," Weis recalled. "What we said is we would start the drive, and, if anything bad happened, we'd just run out the clock."

The Rams had all the momentum, but Belichick was going for it right then. He knew his defense was exhausted, and he trusted Brady not to make the big mistake. Perhaps Belichick remembered the calm, cool, and collected quarterback had fallen asleep on the locker-room floor after arriving at the Louisiana Superdome earlier in the day. After the kickoff, the Patriots had the ball on their own 17. "I think that the Patriots, with this field position, you have to just run the clock out," Madden said. "You have to play for overtime now." There had never been an overtime game in a Super Bowl, and there wouldn't be OT this night.

(That's a story for another day!) Instead, Brady dazzled. He completed 5 passes on the drive, 3 of those to J. R. Redmond, and another, a 23-yarder to Troy Brown that brought the ball into St. Louis territory. "I've been impressed watching Tom Brady. . . . The way he's played in this game today, he has been very, very impressive with his calmness," Madden remarked.

Vinatieri began to loosen up on the Patriots' sideline. Fox flashed a graphic on the television screen that his career long was 55 yards, in 1998. Brady got him closer. With seven seconds to go, the young Patriots QB spiked the ball to stop the clock. "Spiked" is not exactly how Brady handled the situation. He bounced the ball gently, caught it, and handed it to the official. Madden was stunned by the coolness of the gesture. "He just gave me goose bumps," he remarked on the air. It was up to Vinatieri now, from 48 yards. His kick—as time expired—was perfect. The Patriots won, 20–17.

Brady rose to the occasion with the game on the line. The skinny, overlooked backup quarterback coolly and methodically hit on 5 of 8 passes, as New England marched from its 17-yard line to the St. Louis 30, enough to set up Vinatieri's game-winning field goal on the final play of the game.

"I obviously [rate] Tom Brady number one. He continually has success, continually has his team in championship form, [and] continually makes plays in the biggest moments."

—KURT WARNER, HALL OF FAME QB

"You can't say enough about that Brady kid," said wide receiver David Patten. "He has a tremendous amount of confidence, and that allowed him to lead this team. Maybe he didn't have the greatest statistics today, but that doesn't matter. What does matter is that he knows how to win and motivate other players. My hat is off to him." Brady, who had thrown for only 145 yards, didn't care about his numbers, either, because numbers don't attest to his leadership. "What's important is to play your best football when the game is on the line," said Brady, who was named the game's MVP. "We did this against Oakland; we did it at Pittsburgh; and we did it again tonight. We've got a whole team full of underdogs, but now we're the top dogs.

"When I replaced Drew, I was just hoping to get us some wins, and to be a better player at the end of the year than at the beginning," he continued. "Certainly, I'm better, and this is just the icing on what's become a pretty good cake. You dream about this kind of stuff, every player does, but it usually doesn't become reality. This is just amazing, but that's what this team is all about, and I'm just a little piece of the puzzle."

The 2001 NFL season was a magical one for Brady, Belichick, and the Patriots organization. New England won the Super Bowl one year after finishing in the AFC East cellar, with a young Tom Brady, a sixth-round draft pick in 2000, starting the 2001 season as a backup quarterback, and Bill Belichick, who had a losing record in his first six seasons as an NFL head coach with the Cleveland Browns and New England. Despite these incredible accomplishments, Belichick couldn't muster any sentimentality with Brady after claiming their first Super Bowl together. As Brady told it: "He said, 'Tom, just wanted to let you know

Tom Brady celebrating on the podium after the Patriots beat the Rams in Super Bowl XXXVI in New Orleans on February 3, 2002. AP PHOTO / TONY GUTIERREZ

you had a pretty good year.' I said, 'Thanks, Coach.'" Does it get more textbook Belichick than that?

Brady, just twenty-four, was the youngest quarterback to ever win the Super Bowl. During the postgame ceremony, he was standing on a podium, sparkly confetti falling on him like colored rain. In the moment, just five months after the September 11 attacks, owner Robert Kraft held the Vince Lombardi Trophy and stepped to the microphone. "Today," Kraft declared, "we are all Patriots." His words still resonate.

By morning, Brady had been offered the coveted "I'm Going to Disney World!" TV spot and a trip to Orlando. Nonetheless, as per team rules, he had to get his coach's permission to miss the team flight home. "Of course you can go," Belichick said. "How many times do you win the Super Bowl?" The answer, for as long as Brady and Belichick remained together, would always be this: more than anyone ever imagined.

THE MAN

The Patriots returned to New England as conquering heroes. Two days after the triumphant Super Bowl victory, 1.25 million fans lined the streets of Boston for a parade celebrating the franchise's first title since the Boston Patriots, in 1960, and the city's first championship team since the 1986 Boston Celtics. In the aftermath, Brady enjoyed his first taste of being The Man. Here was his full-on embrace of celebrity. He went to Disney World. He won "Best Breakthrough Athlete" at the 2002 ESPY Awards. He was in vogue. He was the glamour boy, dating supermodels and meeting rock musicians. Being the face of an NFL team certainly has its perks, and it's safe to say that Brady enjoyed his share of success both on and off the field.

The combination of his athletic prowess and chiseled good looks created an irresistible treat for the media. The newfound attention turned Brady's personal life into prime celebrity gossip, and he was linked in the press with a number of starlets. His coaches and family watched with a combination of bemusement and concern. Brady struggled to maintain a balance between enjoying himself and drowning in it.

After years of hard work and overcoming countless hurdles, Brady became a household name. Everyone wanted to know more about this new leader, who had improbably turned around a team that finished 5-11 the season before.

Brady was suddenly the face of New England. Everyone in the media wanted a piece of him. Brady was having trouble just saying no to people. Finally, Belichick took him aside and cautioned him on the perils of fame, telling him about how it could alienate him from his fellow players. It was advice that struck a deep chord in Brady.

Even as Brady's popularity reached new heights, he stayed true to his roots. He kept close ties with his family and personal relationships, rather than running wild to soak in the bachelor life. He became the prince of a city and squired some of the world's most beautiful women. Yet he remained a private person, considerate to his fans and respected by teammates and opponents alike. In May, Brady was chosen as one of *People* magazine's 50 Most Beautiful People, and was called the most eligible bachelor in America. "It's very flattering," said Brady. "But, at the same time, I don't think I sleep any better at night being that. No way."

All in all, it was a great year for Serra High School. Lynn Swann was inducted into the Pro Football Hall of Fame. Barry Bonds hit 73 home runs to set a new Major League Baseball single-season home-run record. And now, Tom Brady was the Super Bowl's Most Valuable Player. When he was asked what other people could learn from his dramatic rise from relative obscurity to Super Bowl MVP, his answer mirrored his own life and determined attitude. "Don't let other people tell you what you're capable of," said Brady, who had just transformed the Patriots and changed his life. "Just believe in yourself and keep plugging away and working hard to achieve what you set your mind to. It may not happen within your timetable, but, eventually, you can get it done."

Along with his team, Brady produced a remarkable upset that gifted a beleaguered franchise with an entirely new identity, and that day in New Orleans, the Brady legend was born. The young quarterback, chosen Super Bowl MVP, now stepped into strange new territory. He instantly personified for New Englanders all the hope and optimism for better days ahead.

And now he was the biggest star in America's biggest game.

CHAPTER 7
TOM TERRIFIC

TOM BRADY HAD RISEN FROM RELATIVE OBSCURITY TO SUPER Bowl MVP with incredible swiftness, and he was determined not to slide back toward the abyss of anonymity. He knew that the sports world was littered with players who had abandoned their work ethic after a season of glory and then paid for their lack of effort with a season, or more, of mediocrity. Brady wasn't about to add his name to that list, or take his newfound status as "Tom Terrific" for granted, not even after the Pats had expressed their belief in him by trading Drew Bledsoe to the Buffalo Bills during the 2002 NFL draft.

"If you get to the point where you're complacent, there's always somebody else working hard who's ready to take your job," noted Brady, who wasn't about to allow himself to be sandbagged by a swollen ego or distracted by too many outside interests. "My biggest fear is being a one-hit wonder, so I'm not going to forget who I am or what got me here."

His work habits and commitment to excellence were appreciated by his teammates, who knew how easy it could be for a player, especially a young player who had just tasted his first season of success in the NFL, to lose his focus. "He's been here at seven in the morning, throwing and running throughout the off-season," said Pats' linebacker Larry Izzo. "He works like he's still the sixth-round draft pick trying to make the team, not like he's the Super Bowl MVP. That's why he's become a leader of this team. He earned our respect by working as hard as he does."

Tom Brady scored a rushing touchdown for the first time in his career, against the Tennessee Titans in Nashville, on December 16, 2002.
AP PHOTO / JOHN RUSSELL

When hard-hitting safety Rodney Harrison joined the Patriots prior to the 2003 season, his plan to make a good impression was to outwork everyone. Not that he was always able to. He's told the story of showing up to his first day with the Patriots, hoping to be the first one at the gym. He got there at 7:30 a.m., only to find Brady there in the middle of a workout. So the next day he got there at 7:00, to be greeted by Brady saying, "Good afternoon." The next day, it was 6:30, and Brady was asking if he'd slept in. Harrison, a two-time All-Pro, wasn't going to let that happen again, so he showed up at 6:15 a.m., only to find Brady already there, lifting weights. So the next day Harrison showed up at 6:00. "Good afternoon." Then 5:50. "Good afternoon." Then 5:40. Then 5:30. "Good afternoon" each time, until Harrison finally said, "Screw you, Tom. I'm not coming in any earlier."

> "He has a sickness. He's very competitive and wants that edge all the time to destroy his opponents."
> —DARRELLE REVIS, PRO BOWL DEFENSIVE BACK

When he wasn't working out in preparation for the physical grind of the upcoming season, Brady could usually be found in the film room, where he'd spend five hours a day watching tapes of opposing defenses with his coaches, and then devising strategies to defeat those defenses. David Nugent, a defensive end who shared a condo with Brady, asked him how he could possibly spend five useful hours a day watching tape. "He told me," said Nugent, "When I come up to the line on Sundays, I'll know exactly what I'm facing and how to counteract it because of the time I'm putting in now. The key to being a winning quarterback is preparation.' I have a lot more respect for quarterbacks after rooming with Tom, because I realize how much they have to learn. It's not a position for the unintelligent."

CLOSE DOESN'T CUT IT

All the work that Brady had put in during the off-season was on display at the outset of the 2002 season, as the Patriots posted high-scoring wins over the Steelers, Jets, and Chiefs, whom they defeated in overtime. In those three games,

Brady threw 9 touchdown passes and only 2 interceptions. He started his run in the first game ever played at the new Gillette Stadium by throwing a trio of TD tosses against Pittsburgh, and was named the AFC Offensive Player of the Week. He ended it by ripping the Kansas City secondary for 4 touchdown throws and 410 passing yards. "He's just hit the tip of the iceberg on how good he can really be," said Izzo. "I mean, he still sees that there's a lot of things that he could do better, and just think of where he can go from here after having a great year, a Pro Bowl year. The sky's the limit, and I think he realizes that."

But the early-season fireworks fizzled as New England dropped the next four games. Brady wound up throwing more interceptions than touchdown passes during the losing streak. New England finally stopped the slide with a 38–7 blowout win in Buffalo, as Brady put on a clinic, completing 22 of 26 of his pass attempts, 3 of which went for touchdowns, and was named the Player of the Week for the second time.

The win over the Bills had evened the Pats' record at 4-4 and given them a platform from which to a make a second-half charge at the playoffs. With Brady back on track, New England started their stretch run with a thrilling come-from-behind 33–30 victory at Chicago. The Bears thought they had locked the game away with a 30–19 lead and only 5:22 left to play, but Brady broke their backs by throwing for 2 late touchdowns, including the game-winner to David Patten, which came with only 21 ticks left on the clock.

They came into the final game of the season at Foxborough needing a win over Miami to keep their slim playoff hopes alive. But the Dolphins took it to the Pats and built up a 24–13 lead with less than five minutes left to play in regulation time. And then, just when all seemed lost, Brady turned the game on a dime, by throwing a TD pass to Troy Brown, followed by a 2-point conversion toss to tight end Christian Fauria that cut the deficit to 3 points, with less than three minutes to go. He cashed in another scoring opportunity with a drive that set up Adam Vinatieri's game-tying field goal, and then he hit the jackpot with a drive

Tom Brady plays for championships, not for numbers.

in overtime that positioned Vinatieri's game-winning 3-pointer. The 27–24 win, Brady's fifth-straight OT victory, had upped the Pats' record to 9-7, and a three-way tie for first place in the division with the Dolphins and the Jets. But it was the Jets, based on the NFL's tiebreaker rules, that made it into the postseason, while the Dolphins and the Pats went bust.

Brady had posted a fine follow-up season by throwing for a league-high 28 touchdown passes while finishing third in the AFC, with 3,746 passing yards. But the stats didn't provide any consolation for Brady, who plays for championships, not for numbers. "It was disappointing to come so close, and then not get the opportunity to defend our Super Bowl title," he said. "On the other hand, if we had played better and won another game, we would have been in the playoffs. We just didn't get it done."

TURNING IT AROUND

The Patriots started the 2003 season on the wrong foot when they went to Buffalo and were blown out by the Bills, 31–0, the worst opening-day loss in franchise history. The defeat left an especially sour taste in Brady's mouth, after he was picked off four times and sacked twice. "We've got to play better," he said, "and it starts with me." The team took a step in the right direction the following week, however, by going on the road and defeating the Philadelphia Eagles, 31–10. It was also a personal bounce-back game for Brady, who passed for 3 touchdowns. It was the first time that Brady had shared a field with Donovan McNabb since McNabb had led Syracuse to a dominant victory over Michigan in Brady's second college start.

The Patriots also split their next two games, a win at home against the Jets, followed by a loss in Washington. With a quarter of the season gone, New England was sitting with a 2-2 record, and Brady, with 7 interceptions and only 5 touchdown passes, was as responsible as anyone for the team's mediocre start. The Pats were reeling. The team had missed the playoffs in 2002, and had now lost 9 of 20 games since upsetting the Rams in the Super Bowl.

A COACH'S GAMBLE PAYS OFF

Week 9 of the 2003 season delivered one of the most interesting moments of strategy in NFL history, and it paid off for the Patriots in a memorable *Monday Night Football* game against the Broncos in Denver, which had been a house of horrors for New England entering this prime-time tilt. The Patriots were 1-12 in their last 13 trips to the Mile High City.

New England trailed 24–23 and was pinned at its own 1-yard line in a fourth-down-and-10 situation, with only 2:51 left to play. That's when Bill Belichick made one of the gutsiest moves you'll ever see—he called for an intentional safety. A bold move, but one that made sense, because all New England needed for the plan to work was a quick defensive stop. And that's exactly what happened.

The defense held Denver to a three-and-out, and put the ball back in Tom Brady's hands at his own 42-yard line, with 2:15 still on the clock. On the ensuing drive, Brady completed 3 passes to halfback Kevin Faulk for 40 yards, and capped it off with an 18-yard strike to wide receiver David Givens on a back shoulder throw in the front of the end zone, to give the Patriots a 30–26 victory. But it wouldn't have been possible without Belichick's gamble.

Suddenly, though, the team jelled, Brady got hot, and the Patriots ran the table, winning all of their remaining 12 games to finish atop the AFC East with an NFL-best 14-2 record. The run started with a hard-fought 38–30 win over the Tennessee Titans, and there were a number of other games along the way when the streak was almost ended. The first near-loss occurred in Miami, two weeks after the Titans game, but Brady stepped up and saved the day by connecting on an 82-yard pass play with Troy Brown that gave the Pats a 19–13 overtime win. Two weeks later, Brady led New England to a come-from-behind 30–26 win in Denver when he teamed up with wide receiver David Givens on a game-winning scoring connection, with only eighteen seconds left to play. The throw completed an exquisite game for Brady, who threw for 350 yards and 3 touchdowns, adding yet another Player of the Week honor to a crowded mantel.

Tom Brady and Bill Belichick hug it out following their second Super Bowl title together. AP PHOTO / DAVID J. PHILLIP

Brady also rode to the rescue in Houston when, with forty seconds remaining in the fourth quarter, he threw a short, game-tying touchdown pass to tight end Daniel Graham. The Pats then went on to beat the Texans in OT, which improved Brady's record in overtime games to a perfect 7-0. New England finished the regular season run with a 31–0 blowout win over Buffalo, a mirror image of their opening-day loss. It was also a stunning reversal from that first game for Brady, who passed for a season-high 4 touchdowns and . . . yeah, he was Player of the Week again. Brady finished the season with another set of impressive stats and his second invitation in three years to the Pro Bowl, but, more importantly, the Patriots had made it back into postseason play, and he was going to have the opportunity to try for a second Super Bowl ring.

New England started its playoff drive at Foxborough with a rematch against the Titans, who were led by quarterback Steve McNair, the NFL's co-MVP in 2003. The second game was different from the first one in almost every way, beginning with the bone-chilling 4-degree weather at kickoff. In addition to numbing the players, the cold also made the ball slick and hard to grip, so, unlike the first game, this one turned into a gritty defensive struggle. With the teams knotted at 14–14 deep into the fourth quarter, Brady, who had thrown for the Pats' first score and set up the second with his passing, led New England on a short drive down to the Titans' 27-yard line. When the drive stalled, Vinatieri came into the game and split the uprights with a kick that sent New England into the AFC Championship Game against Indianapolis.

Vinatieri also played a major role in the Patriots' win the following week, by kicking 5 field goals at Foxborough, as New England ended the Colts' season with a 24–14 win. Indianapolis had made it into the title game behind the passing of Peyton Manning, who had thrown 8 touchdown passes in the team's playoff wins over Denver and Kansas City. But the New England defense, which had been superb throughout the season, stifled Manning, who had shared NFL MVP honors with McNair, and picked off 4 of his passes.

> "He's the greatest of all time. I don't care what anyone says."
> —BOOMER ESIASON, NFL MVP QB

Although Brady hadn't been especially sharp or produced great stats, he had, once again, showed that he could somehow do enough to win a big game. "Tom Brady is the greatest winner in football right now, I don't care what anybody says," said cornerback Ty Law, who had intercepted Manning three times. "Maybe his numbers aren't always eye-popping, but he knows how to win ball games. Those other quarterbacks, with all their awards and stats, are sitting at home. I'll play with Tom any day."

Though he was not yet a great pure passer, Brady proved to be an excellent leader. "The mark of a great player is how well you play over time," Brady said. "That's the goal—to be dependable, to be consistent." His teammates knew they could most depend on Brady in the playoffs. He helped them beat Tennessee in the bitter cold, then Indianapolis, to reach the Super Bowl. Once there, it was time for Tom to be terrific.

"MOVING UP THE LADDER"

The Patriots were holding an intrasquad scrimmage a few days before Super Bowl XXXVIII in preparation for their opponent, the upstart Carolina Panthers. Competition between New England's offensive and defensive units, even in practice, is typically fierce. Brady threw an interception to teammate Rodney Harrison and the quarterback, already in his Super Bowl mind-set, wasn't pleased with the result. He chased after Harrison, screaming expletives. "Practice is a game situation [for Brady]," said Harrison, whose 30.5 career sacks is an NFL record for a player at his position. "His personality is the same in practice as it is in the game. He's fiery. He's intense."

The game played at Houston's Reliant Stadium was a defensive-minded 14–10 contest until a wild fourth quarter, when the teams combined for 37 points. The most surprising 6 points came courtesy of linebacker Mike Vrabel—on offense—on a goal-line touchdown catch. Vrabel, who had been brought in on the play as an extra tight end, released into the end zone and easily caught the score to put New England up 29–22

Tom Brady now was a celebrity, scoring invites to the White House and to Disney World.

with 2:51 remaining. "Touchdowns are always bigger than sacks, especially in the Super Bowl," said Vrabel, who caught another touchdown in the Super Bowl against the Eagles the next year. "They're few and far between."

The wild fourth quarter included heroics by wide receiver Deion Branch, who recorded 10 receptions for 143 yards and a touchdown. Branch's last catch came on the game's final drive on a play beginning at Carolina's 40-yard line with

Tom Brady's unbelievable good fortune resulted in two Super Bowl wins in his first three years as the Patriots' quarterback. AP PHOTO / DAVE MARTIN

fourteen seconds left on the clock. Tied 29–29, Brady found Branch near the sideline for a 17-yard gain to put the Patriots in field-goal range for kicker Adam Vinatieri, who remarked on the final drive: "If you ever give us time, look out." There was no panic in Vinatieri and probably not much doubt on either sideline that he was going to break the 29–29 tie with under ten seconds left when he lined up for the kick. "The team knew [Vinatieri] was going to make the kick," said linebacker Ted Johnson. "He's the Iceman and he never misses when the game is on the line."

Of course, Vinatieri nailed it and the Patriots won, 32–29.

"This team has met all comers," Belichick said of the team's performance and climactic finish. "That's 15 straight [victories]. We caused some heart attacks, but we came out on top."

Brady was named Super Bowl MVP when it was all over. He led three scoring drives of 68 yards or longer, setting up another one of the most memorable winning kicks in recent history. He completed 32 of 48 passes for 354 yards and 3 touchdowns. Tom Terrific had now racked up two Super Bowl appearances, two championships, and two Super Bowl MVPs in three years—and he was just getting started. "Tom's moving up the ladder of the league's best quarterbacks," said Belichick. "He deserves to be mentioned with all the best quarterbacks. Tom's a winner."

Tom Brady now was a celebrity, scoring invites to the White House and to Disney World. He soon would be hosting TV shows and appearing in national commercials. "It's been a great couple of years," he said. "But when that success on the football field goes away, so do all the really neat things I get to do. That's why football is always going to be No. 1."

MR. INCREDIBLE

The Patriots started the 2004 season with six straight victories, which upped their consecutive-game-winning streak to 21, a new NFL record. During the streak, the Pats won 13 games at home, 7 on the road, and 1, the Super Bowl in Houston, on a neutral field. For his part, over those 21 straight wins, Brady passed for 34 touchdowns and threw only 12 interceptions. The winning streak came to a decisive end in Pittsburgh, however, when the Steelers defeated the Patriots on Halloween, 34–20. The goblins certainly seemed to get to Brady, who coughed up a fumble and threw a pair of interceptions. But the Patriots bounced right back and won 8 of their final 9 games, to finish the season at 14-2 for the second successive year, and capture the AFC East title for the third time in Brady's four seasons as the team's starter.

New England began the postseason part of its Super Bowl defense by again hosting Indianapolis, who had led the NFL in scoring by a vast margin. Peyton Manning, who was named the league MVP again, had crafted an incredible year, passing for an NFL-record 49 touchdowns, 1 more than Dan Marino had thrown for the Dolphins in 1984. He'd continued his amazing aerial act in Indianapolis's opening-round playoff game by lighting up the Broncos with 4 more touchdown passes, and the Colts came into Foxborough under a full head of steam after defeating Denver, 49–24.

"You're not going to stop them," said Denver coach Mike Shanahan. "You just have to try to slow them down. And the only way to slow them down is to keep them off the field." But New England's defense stopped the Colts in their tracks; paving the way for a 20–3 Patriots win. Brady, meanwhile, threw for one score and ran for another. "He's incredible," said tight end Christian Fauria. "He's never yet let us down."

> "People don't realize how hard it is to be consistent. That's why you give a lot of credit to Tom Brady and the Patriots."
>
> —DONOVAN MCNABB, PRO BOWL QB

The Patriots had to travel to Heinz Field to play the AFC Championship Game in Pittsburgh, where their 21-game winning streak had been brought to an end three months earlier. The Steelers had gone on to post an NFL-best 15-1 record during the regular season. Offensively, the Steelers were led by a grinding running game and by quarterback Ben Roethlisberger, who had piloted Pittsburgh to 14 straight wins, and was named the NFL Offensive Rookie of the Year. On the other side of the line of scrimmage, the Steelers had created a modern-day version of their legendary Steel Curtain defense, and it had been the stingiest unit in the NFL, allowing only 15.6 points per game.

But it was the New England defense that set the tone early by picking off Roethlisberger's first pass. Brady had a fever above 100 degrees and spent the night before the game sick in bed with the flu. Nonetheless, he went right at the Steelers' defense and opened the scoring with a 60-yard touchdown strike to Deion Branch. After Brady had led New England on two additional first-half scoring drives, Rodney Harrison stepped in front of another Roethlisberger pass and turned it into an 87-yard touchdown return that opened the Patriots lead to 24–3 at halftime. After the intermission, Brady flawlessly guided the Patriots to 17 second-half points and a 41–24 victory. In what was one of the coldest games

Hail to the victors, from left: Troy Brown, Rodney Harrison, Richard Seymour, Tedy Bruschi, Tom Brady, and Robert Kraft show off the bling. AP PHOTO / ADAM HUNGER

ever at Heinz Field, Brady was 14 for 21 for 207 yards, 2 touchdowns, and 0 interceptions.

"It's amazing to watch," said Pats linebacker Ted Johnson, referring to Brady's errorless performance. "There are other outstanding quarterbacks, but he just has an uncanny ability to rise up at the most critical times. And he does it time after time."

After the game, when some reporters tried to make too much of his illness, Brady got annoyed with them. "It wasn't a big deal, and I don't want it to take away from what everyone else on the team has accomplished," he explained. "Everyone else plays with toughness and never complains. Guys in our locker room have played with broken bones." Brady also became a bit testy when he was asked what he thought about his 8-0 record in playoff games. "There are a bunch of guys in this locker room who are 8-0, and I'm just one of them," he noted. "But we're all proud to be going back to the Super Bowl for a second year in a row."

THREE OUT OF FOUR

The day after the AFC Championship Game ended, Brady was in the film room, watching tape of the Philadelphia Eagles, who would be New England's opponent in Super Bowl XXXIX. Typically, he would watch tape until 11:00 at night and be in the weight room the following morning at 6:30, before any of his teammates had even finished their breakfast. "The rest of us were still eating scrambled eggs," Rodney Harrison cracked. "Tom is always preparing, always working to gain that extra edge."

For Brady, putting in all the work that he does allows him to go into games with confidence, knowing that he, with a great deal of help from his coaches, has solved the riddle of opposing defenses and knows how to exploit their weaknesses. "There's no reason to be worried," said Brady, who was so relaxed before Super Bowl XXXVI that he had fallen asleep in the locker room on game day. "I feel like I'm going into the test with all the answers."

Of course, there are things in life that can't be prepared for, as Brady was reminded of when his ninety-four-year-old grandmother, Margaret Brady, passed away on the Wednesday night before the Super Bowl. "She had been ill for quite some time, but things suddenly took a turn for the worse," said Brady. "Hopefully, I can live to be ninety-four and have a full life like she did."

Although Brady was as prepared as he could be when the Patriots ran onto the floodlit field of Jacksonville's Alltel Stadium to take on the Eagles in Super Bowl XXXIX, he knew that he was going up against the NFC's top-rated defensive unit and a secondary that was sending three of its four members to the Pro Bowl. Brady would have liked to get the jump on that formidable defense by putting points on the scoreboard quickly, but it was the Eagles who struck first, as Donovan McNabb capped a long second-quarter drive with a 6-yard touchdown pass to tight end L. J. Smith.

The New England offense, which had been stymied throughout the first half, finally started to move, and Brady led them on a drive deep into Philadelphia territory. With the ball on the Eagles' four, Brady backpedaled and, after looking left and checking off his two primary receivers, found David Givens in the right corner of the end zone for the game-tying touchdown pass, seventy-six seconds before halftime.

Brady went right to work in the second half, teaming with Branch on 3 big passing plays, and then lofting a 2-yard touchdown pass to Mike Vrabel that put the Patriots ahead, 14–7. But McNabb answered back by leading the Eagles on a 10-play, 74-yard drive that he capped with a 10-yard scoring pass to running back Brian Westbrook, tying the score at 14–14 with 3:35 left in the third quarter. The New England offense, which had been so docile for most of the first half, roared right back into action with scoring drives on its next 2 possessions, which upped the Patriots' lead to 24–14, with 8:43 left to play. "Hands down, he's the best we've faced," said Eagles strong safety Mike Lewis. "I don't know another quarterback in the league who plays at his level."

The Eagles later narrowed the Pats' lead to 24–21 on a McNabb touchdown pass with 1:55 left in the game. But that was as close as Philadelphia came, because Rodney Harrison picked off McNabb's last desperate pass with ten seconds left, securing New England's third Super Bowl victory in four years. But when the talk turned to the word *dynasty*, the Patriots seemed totally uninterested.

"We started at the bottom of the mountain with everyone else and we're happy to get to the top," said Belichick. "I'll leave the historical perspectives to everyone else." Brady, whose ninth consecutive playoff win had tied the NFL record set by the former Green Bay quarterback, Bart Starr, was equally unconcerned with discussions about dynasties. "If you guys in the media say we're a great team, then we accept the compliment," said Brady. "But we just love playing football. It's as simple as that. We love to play the game, and we play it like it's supposed to be played—as a team."

Tom Brady had been the Patriots' starting quarterback over the previous four years, and the Patriots had won three championships by a total of 9 points. In two of three Super Bowls that they'd won, he'd been the MVP. Now Brady would forever be discussed in the same conversation with the greatest quarterbacks who'd ever played. He no longer was the scrappy sixth-round pick; he was now being spoken of in the company of legendary quarterbacks like his idol, Joe Montana, and Terry Bradshaw, and Bart Starr. He also would be held up as the ideal player on an exemplary team. It was the 21-game winning streak and the third Super Bowl win over the Eagles that cemented the Patriots, and Tom Brady, as the model of NFL excellence.

CHAPTER 8
FACE OF A DYNASTY

THE NEW ENGLAND PATRIOTS, WINNERS OF THREE SUPER Bowls in four years, had, without question, proven they were a superior franchise, and Tom Brady had already established himself as one of the NFL's brightest stars. For his next star turn, he went to New York to host *Saturday Night Live*. Hitting the stage shortly after the Patriots won Super Bowl XXXIX, the telegenic QB awkwardly (yet charmingly) participated in sketches that poked fun at his clean-cut image. He opened his monologue with a bit that required him to dance and sing a mockingly boastful song. Insisting he can sing even though he can't hold a tune, Brady crooned the immortal couplet: "I won the Tour de France, and I did it with no pants. So when I rode by, you saw my sweet behind."

In typical Brady fashion, he involved himself in all aspects of the production. During rehearsals, however, there was a skit involving the Philadelphia Eagles, whom the Patriots had defeated in the Super Bowl three months earlier. The sketch was cut at Brady's request because he was worried it might be disrespectful to an opponent. He was willing to make fun of himself, but he didn't want to upset anyone else. The quarterback continued to display his comedic chops on TV, guest-starring as himself on *The Simpsons* and *Family Guy*. He also made very funny cameo appearances in the films *Ted 2* and *Entourage*.

The long-running show of success by the Patriots continued when the team unveiled a third championship banner before kicking off the 2005 schedule. New England welcomed the Oakland Raiders—making their first visit to Foxborough

Tom Brady, with game face on, before the start of Super Bowl LII, on February 4, 2018. AP PHOTO / MATT SLOCUM

since the infamous Tuck Rule incident in the Snow Bowl playoff game—to Gillette Stadium for a Thursday-night season kickoff game. Brady threw 2 touchdown passes as the Patriots opened their quest for an unprecedented third straight Super Bowl victory by beating Oakland, 30–20. New England's thirty-fifth win in thirty-nine games since the start of the 2003 season was a bit of a freak show. It started with Ozzy Osbourne and his heavy metal band putting on a pregame concert for the prime-time crowd. The former Black Sabbath front man performed his wild-and-woolly song "Crazy Train" on a stage within a giant football helmet that had opened to reveal the Ozzman wearing a Patriots No. 1 jersey, mugging for the cameras and singing with a keen abandon.

New England got off to a rocky start to the season, just 4-4 at the halfway mark. One of the fretful losses came at the hands of the San Diego Chargers, who had come into Foxborough and ended the Patriots' 21-game home winning streak with a 41–17 blowout. The 41 points were the most scored against New England in nearly seven years. At a particularly frustrating moment, Brady fired a water bottle to the ground and screamed that he wasn't going to accept losing. "He is a fiery guy," said Charlie Weis, a coach who worked very closely with Brady before leaving for Notre Dame. "He's a get-in-your-face yeller and hollerer, but he also has such a calm demeanor at the line of scrimmage. There's an air about him. You know something good is going to happen."

Brady had, in fact, continued to make good things happen, and he had been the main reason the Patriots had split the first eight games. Now he was finding a rhythm in the high-tempo offense installed by offensive coordinator Josh McDaniels, and feeling more in sync with his new coach. By season's end, Brady was the league's leading passer for the first time in his career, surpassing 4,000 yards, to go along with 4 game-winning fourth-quarter drives. The most electric comeback was staged in Miami. Tight end Ben Watson caught

> "You can make an argument that he's the best player that ever walked."
>
> —JASON GARRETT, FORMER NFL HEAD COACH

touchdown passes of 16 and 17 yards from Brady to pace New England's 23–16 victory over the Dolphins in Week 10. The Dolphins had taken a 16–15 lead with 2:59 remaining in the game. After the ensuing kickoff, Brady needed just 2 pass plays to cover 76 yards of field position—in thirty-four seconds—to put the Patriots back on top. "I think I've grown into the role the coaches have given me," said Brady, who made All-Pro for the first time as an encore.

The Pats finished strong in 2005, winning 6 of 8, and clinched the AFC East title for a third successive season. Through the high notes and lows, Brady had stood tall as one of the team's few constants, and when they needed him most, he had, arguably, delivered his finest season to date. "He brings so much to our team with his preparation, his work ethic, his toughness, and his ability to lead our offense," said Belichick. "I'm very glad that he's our quarterback."

Tom Brady is an accomplished practical joker and more mischievous than he appears. AP PHOTO / CHARLES KRUPA

THE GOAT

A few days before the season-opener with Oakland, Brady appeared in *GQ* magazine. He was photographed in fashionable clothes, even donning a yachting cap. During the photo shoot, which took place on a farm, somebody handed Brady a baby goat. A picture with a kid was sure to catch the attention of his teammates. The day after that issue hit the newsstands, Brady practiced with the team. He broke the huddle, brought the team up to the line of scrimmage, and discovered that tackle Matt Light and center Dan Koppen had pinned the goat photo to the backs of their jerseys. No one laughed harder than Brady. The incident mirrored another prank played on Brady after he hosted *Saturday Night Live*. He performed one skit in his underwear. After the show aired, he found the Patriots locker room festooned with Jockey shorts.

As a team, the Patriots don't show much personality in public. Bill Belichick's press conferences are about as amusing as a computer virus. Inside the locker room, however, when the television cameras are out of sight and reporters' note-pads have been put away, the players love to joke around. The Patriots really can be a loose, trash-talking, fun-loving bunch. And the quarterback is the team leader in this category, too. Brady, who is more mischievous than he appears, is one of the most accomplished practical jokers the NFL has seen in a long time. Known as the Patriots' resident prankster, he once paid to have all four tires removed from backup quarterback Matt Cassel's car. Three tires were stacked in front of Cassel's locker, the fourth, hidden in the trainer's room.

> "I think Tom is the greatest to ever have played the game because he's been able to do it with so many people revolving around him."
> —JOE THEISMANN, NFL MVP QB

To retaliate, Cassel found Brady's Nike shoes in his locker and filled them with shaving cream. When Brady came in to get dressed after a post-practice shower, he put his sneakers on and his feet were buried in foam. Sensing an opportunity, Light and Koppen filled Brady's car with Styrofoam packing peanuts. They opened the sunroof of Brady's Lexus and poured in three industrial-size bags, filling the interior of Brady's ride to the brim.

"We couldn't get one more peanut in there," Light recounted. The linemen thought they were framing Cassel, but Brady was on to them. By the time practice was over, his car was vacuumed and cleaned out. Brady, always a good sport, decided it was best not to retaliate. "I wanted them to get the last laugh," he said. Belichick caught wind of the prank war after the packing-peanuts episode, and he was not happy, calling for a moratorium on the practical jokes. "Let's not let this get out of hand," he told the players.

JABAR
GAFFNEY 10

Tom Brady's weekly media sessions are a main event, with crowds spilling over in front of neighboring lockers. AP PHOTO / STEPHAN SAVOIA

Brady is extremely popular in the locker room, and highly respected by team-mates, who have elected him as an offensive captain every year since 2002. There are quarterbacks whose standing with their teammates never would have survived all the individual attention, whose images as matinee idols and pub-lic figures would have put their football credibility into question. Those quarterbacks would have been scorned by teammates. But that didn't happen to Brady. In his career with the Patriots, Brady has never talked about individual achievement. It's always about the team. A pro football team is very much a fam-ily; its players form a brotherhood, and Brady revels in the jocularity. "All I ever wanted was the camaraderie, to share some memories with so many other guys," he said. "I mean, if you choose to alienate yourself or put yourself apart, you know, play tennis. Play golf."

Brady always has defined himself as part of a team.

Millions of young women have a strong interest in Brady's personal life and romantic interests. He has over 1.8 million followers to his Twitter account and nearly 9.5 million on Instagram, due, in part, to his broad appeal. The dimpled, clean-cut quarterback caused hearts to flutter with girlfriend Bridget Moynahan on his arm upon arrival at the Los Angeles premiere of the actress's new film, the science-fiction thriller *I, Robot*, co-starring Will Smith, on July 7, 2004. The quar-terback had met the actress earlier in the year. They dated for over two years and then called it quits. Soon enough, Brady had a new squeeze, Gisele Bündchen, a Brazilian supermodel. The pair had met on a blind date following the model's appearance on *The Ellen DeGeneres Show*. Bündchen told *Vanity Fair* it was love at first sight. "I knew right away," she said. "The moment I saw him, he smiled, and I was like, 'That is the most beautiful, charismatic smile I've ever seen!' "

The highly successful Victoria's Secret model and new face of the NFL turned their rendezvous into true love. But just as things were heating up for the new couple, Brady's ex-girlfriend discovered she was expecting a baby. The fact that Brady and Moynahan had already split, and he had already moved on to a new love interest, only made the public's fascination with the state of affairs that much more intense. Their love triangle became a hot topic on social media—it's easy to understand how the public lives of three impossibly good-looking people might be turned into a soap opera—and Brady's all-American image took a bit of a hit.

The experience caused Brady to think carefully about what he posts on social media to his fans. "I think, I try to make mine a reflection of who I am and what I care about," he said. However, he's aware that any mistakes could be costly for his image. "As a public figure there's a responsibility to try to do the right thing," he added. "Life is challenging. I don't think anybody is perfect." Luckily, everything worked out in the end. Brady and Moynahan decided to raise a child together. The actress gave birth to son Jack in August 2007, and while it hasn't always been easy, Moynahan says she and Brady make a winning team when it comes to co-parenting their child. "My son is surrounded by love," said the actress, best known for her role on television's *Blue Bloods*. "I don't think you can ask for more than that."

BRADY-MANIA

Brady-mania was sweeping the nation. Sportscasters heaped praise on his field generalship. Young women everywhere thought he was dreamy. Parents liked him, too. "Every mother and father in New England wants their daughter to be dating Tom Brady," said teammate Larry Izzo. It seemed everyone was clamoring for the fresh-faced quarterback. Brady was a judge for the Miss USA Pageant; his face beamed down from billboards for the "Got Milk?" ad campaigns; and he was named one of *People* magazine's 50 Most Beautiful People. He was even invited to be a special guest at the White House for President George W. Bush's State of the Union address in 2004.

Brady had become the NFL's rock star, as much The Boss as Bruce Springsteen. As such, he came into great demand. His weekly media sessions had become such major events that the crowd spilled over in front of neighboring lockers. The situation got so unwieldy that teammates couldn't get at their shoes or their pants. Due to the unprecedented media crush that resulted from his success, and that of the team, by the beginning of the 2005 season, the Patriots' public relations staff moved Brady's interviews into the Gillette Stadium media room, where he met the press and took questions planted behind a wooden podium. This was a problem for Brady because it set him apart from his teammates. "Some people are comfortable behind the podium," he said. "But I don't need to be the show-stopper, the entertainer. I'd much rather people assume I'm one of the guys."

Brady always has defined himself as part of a team, and the quarterback, ever conscientious, seemed to be handling his celebrity status with the same self-assured, cool approach he has toward playing football. Earlier in the year, Brady had signed a new six-year contract worth nearly $60 million, which was considerably less money than market price for a quarterback with three rings, so the Patriots would have maneuvering room under the salary cap. "Is it going to make me feel any better to make an extra million?" he wondered. "That million might be more important to the team."

With the outside noise from the regular season in his rearview mirror, Brady was looking forward to the playoffs and hoping the Patriots could become the first team in NFL history to win three straight Super Bowls. The Patriots began the postseason with a 28–3 victory over the Jacksonville Jaguars. Tom Terrific threw 3 touchdown passes, 1 each to Troy Brown, David Givens, and Ben Watson, who took a short pass and turned it into a spectacular 63-yard score. "Tom Brady just seems to have a knack for knowing what to do in every situation," said Reggie Hayward, a Jacksonville defensive end. "He knows how to handle whatever defenses are called against them, and he knows when to check off a play and call an audible. He just knows the game."

The win over Jacksonville was the Patriots' tenth-straight postseason victory, an NFL record, but even before the players left the field, they were already thinking about the next steps on the path toward the Super Bowl. "It's a great accomplishment," said linebacker Willie McGinest, the NFL's leader in postseason sacks, with 16. "We're not downplaying it, but they're not passing out any trophies tonight. We've got a long way to go."

Tom Brady accepting the Sports Illustrated *Sportsman of the Year award with his parents, Tom Brady Sr. and Galynn, in New York on December 6, 2005.* AP PHOTO / HENNY RAY ABRAMS

New England's dream of an unprecedented third straight title fizzled in Denver with a disappointing 27–13 loss to the Broncos in the AFC Championship Game. In reality, the Patriots beat themselves. After winning 10 straight playoff games with only 6 turnovers, New England, with 3 fumbles and 2 interceptions, turned the ball over 5 times. In fact, all but 3 of Denver's points were the result of New England miscues. A team that had rarely beaten itself, and never in the postseason, had all at once become sloppier than anyone could have imagined. "When you lose, you want to at least go down fighting," said Brady. "You want to go down playing your best, but we didn't do that. We made it easy for them."

The pain from the loss in the conference championship game lingered with the fans of New England throughout the off-season, like a dull ache in the back of

one's brain. What hurt so much was not the final score, but the knowledge that the team had failed to perform up to its abilities, and had played so poorly in such a big game. "Realistically, we know that we're not going to win every game or capture every Super Bowl," acknowledged Brady. "But there's a difference between being beaten and beating yourself. We could live with being beaten, but beating yourself is a lot harder to deal with."

Although the team had fallen short of its goal, the accolades for Brady continued to come pouring in. In December, he was formally presented with *Sports Illustrated*'s Sportsman of the Year award at the Time Warner Center in New York. A taped message of tribute came from U2's Bono, who congratulated Brady by joking: "It doesn't get much better than being on the cover of *Sports Illustrated*'s Swimsuit Issue. . . . I then learned that it's [the] Sportsman of the Year issue. I know, Tom, that it must be a big disappointment for you." Belichick said of the well-deserved honor: "I would just add maybe Person of the Year. His makeup, his character, and the way he carries himself on and off the field, in and out of football, is, I think, exemplary in all phases."

The win in San Diego marked the sixth time Brady led a postseason fourth-quarter comeback.

The last pro football player to receive the magazine's Sportsman of the Year award was the 49ers' Joe Montana, in 1990. Brady, who was raised outside of San Francisco, and whose family had 49ers' season tickets, has often said that he grew up idolizing Montana. By one measure, Brady already had bettered Montana— and every other quarterback. At twenty-eight, he had won three Super Bowls at a younger age than any quarterback in history.

The year was a grand showcase for the two-time Super Bowl MVP. Already in 2005, Brady had hosted *Saturday Night Live*, and he'd been profiled by ESPN's *SportsCentury* and *60 Minutes*. He had been the lead in national commercials, and *Sports Illustrated* had named him its Sportsman of the Year. He also was dating Gisele Bündchen, the gorgeous Victoria's Secret supermodel. Tom Brady was at the top of his profession. And he was just coming into his prime.

THE CARDIAC KIDS

If there was a plus side to losing in Denver one game shy of qualifying for the Super Bowl, it was the way the Patriots used their disappointment to fuel their motivation for the 2006 season. But some of the players who had played especially important roles on the team were no longer there. Most notably, Adam Vinatieri, who had kicked so many game-winning field goals for New England, had signed with the Indianapolis Colts. Even without Vinatieri, who was capably replaced by rookie Stephen Gostkowski, the Patriots began the season with a bang, winning 6 of their first 7 games, and Brady, looking as sharp as he ever had, led the way with 14 touchdown passes. They did hit a slight speed bump with losses over the following two weeks, but New England went right back to their winning ways, and closed out the regular season the same way they had started it, by taking 6 of their final 7 games.

The Patriots, by virtue of a 12-4 record that put the team in its accustomed spot atop the AFC East standings, was now prepared to focus all its attention on the playoffs. The opening-round opponent, the division-rival New York Jets, came into Gillette Stadium to give the hometown favorites all that they could handle, and for one half, they did just that. But New England outscored New York in the second half for a 37–16 win going away. The Patriots then flew to the West Coast for their next step on the playoff ladder, where their reward for beating the Jets was a showdown against the San Diego Chargers, who had finished the regular season with an NFL-best 14-2 record.

The Chargers, who had led the league in scoring, were widely considered to be the most talented team in the tournament and were favored to go all the way and win their first Super Bowl. The Patriots, though, had played against and beaten other talented teams on their way to three Super Bowl titles, so they weren't about to be intimidated by the prospect of playing against the Chargers, or any other team. Brady, however, threw 3 interceptions in a postseason game for the first time in his career. He wasn't able to rise to the expectations that he had created by his performances in previous playoff games—at least, not until the final minutes of the fourth quarter, when the Patriots trailed the Chargers, 21–13, and looked as though they were headed for an early vacation.

The comeback started right after the darkest moment of the day for the Patriots, when Morton McRee picked off a Brady pass and turned upfield. During McRee's return, however, Troy Brown stripped the ball away, and it was recovered at the San Diego 32-yard line by Patriots' wide receiver Reche Caldwell. Brady capitalized with a quick touchdown pass to Caldwell. The Pats added a 2-point conversion to tie the score at 21, with 4:36 showing on the scoreboard clock.

After a three-and-out by the Chargers, the ball was back in Brady's hands for New England's final drive of the game, starting at its own 15-yard line with 3:30 left to play. Brady completed a 19-yard pass to Daniel Graham at the 34 and then misfired twice. Facing third-down-and-10, the Patriots were in the unenviable position of having to make a first down or punt

> "I think Tom Brady's the greatest quarterback to ever play in the league. If you look at the records, they back it up."
>
> —JIMMY JOHNSON, HALL OF FAME COACH

the ball back to the Chargers. That's when Brady made the play of the day, hitting Caldwell in full stride racing down the far right sideline for a key 49-yard completion to the San Diego 17. Three plays later, Gostkowski came out and calmly split the uprights with a 31-yard field goal that gave the Patriots a 24–21 lead with 1:10 left in the game—the first time they had been in front since leading 3–0.

Brady, who has been the hero of so many dramatic Patriots' playoff victories, put up 11 points in less than three and a half minutes against a stunned Chargers team. The wild comebacks drove his father crazy. "He never wins a game 42–10 and so we can just sit back and relax," said Tom Sr. "Everything goes down to the last drive. It's great for cardiologists. It's not great for parents." It's also miserable for opposing teams, who have yet to find a cure for Brady's hammer. "His record speaks for itself," said San Diego head coach Norv Turner. "He just finds a way to get it done over and over and over again. I don't think there's any situation that he hasn't mastered. He's a great decision-maker. You don't want to get into a two-minute drill against Brady."

NO MORE RABBITS

The win sent New England to Indianapolis for the AFC Championship Game against the Colts and Peyton Manning, the perennial Pro Bowl quarterback. Manning had already amassed an amazing pile of passing records, but he would have been willing to trade every one of his records for any one of Brady's three Super Bowl wins. The Patriots had done as much as any team to block the Colts' path to a championship, having knocked them off in two previous postseason meetings since Brady had come on the scene. And, for the first half of this game, it looked as though it was going to be more of the same, as the Patriots came out strong. New England scored touchdowns 53 seconds apart early in the second quarter to take a commanding 21–3 lead. There was still 9:25 left in the second quarter, so there was plenty of time, but no team had ever come from 18 points down in a conference championship game.

The Colts, though, came roaring out of their RCA Dome locker room for the second half, and Manning brought his team back even at 21–21, with four minutes left in the third quarter. Then it was back-and-forth action. Vinatieri, who ended up three-for-three in field-goal attempts for the Colts, kicked a 36-yarder with 5:35 to play that knotted the game at 31–31. New England quickly regained the lead, however, as a 41-yard kickoff return by Ellis Hobbs set them up at their own 46-yard line. From there, Brady connected on a 25-yard pass to Daniel Graham and, when the drive stalled due to a key dropped pass by Reche Caldwell in the end zone, Gostkowski split the uprights to give the Patriots a 34–31 lead, with 3:49 left on the clock.

This time, though, the defense did not hold, as it had in the Chargers game, and countless other games. Manning led the Colts on an 80-yard touchdown drive that put them in the lead, 38–34, with 1:02 left to play. This time, the Comeback Kid didn't have any rabbits to pull out of his hat. Instead, the game ended as the previous year's playoff loss to Denver had, with Brady throwing an interception. "It's always sour when it ends," said Brady. "The competitive part of you always wants it to end at the Super Bowl. But we'll come back next year and try to do it better."

There wasn't much more Tom Brady could have done better. In his first six seasons as New England's starting quarterback, he had already put himself on the road to the Pro Football Hall of Fame. He became the fourth quarterback to lead his team to three or more Super Bowl wins in a career. The other three who did it—Terry Bradshaw and Joe Montana, who won four titles each, and Troy Aikman, who won three Super Bowl championships—are all enshrined in the Hall of Fame. Although Brady bowed out of the playoff picture in the previous two seasons earlier than he would have liked, or had become accustomed to, his 12-2 record and .857 winning percentage in postseason play was still the best of any quarterback in history, except for Bart Starr, who posted a 9-1 record and a .900 winning percentage.

Brady's playoff magic led to comparisons with Joe Montana, his boyhood sports idol, because Brady, like Montana, was known for maintaining his cool when the stakes and the heat were raised, and for winning multiple Super Bowls. Even Bill Walsh, the Hall of Fame coach, who drafted and coached Montana, saw a similarity. "He's as close to Joe as anyone I've ever seen," said Walsh. "Joe was unique, but I certainly see echoes of him in Tom."

Montana has also expressed his admiration for Brady's ability and composure. "I just like watching him play, and seeing how he carries himself," said the man with the nickname Joe Cool. "He's always in control, and always doing the right thing. I think he's in a position to win a lot more championships, but it won't get easier. He'll find there is no end to the expectations."

Brady, meanwhile, deflected the praise and comparisons, and the talk about his place in football history. "I'm very flattered, but I don't think I'm on that level; I'm still trying to get better," said Brady. "[W]hat a great thing that would be, to play like one of the best quarterbacks of all time. But, I think I'm a long ways from that. I hope those comparisons are still around at the end of my career."

CHAPTER 9
IN PURSUIT OF PERFECTION

TOM BRADY AND THE NEW ENGLAND PATRIOTS SET OUT TO defy expectations of what is possible in professional sports. During the 2007 season, the Patriots averaged 37 points a game, allowed just 17, and scored 48 or more points four times. Tom Terrific officially became known as Touchdown Tom, as he passed for a mind-boggling 50 touchdowns in the regular season, setting a new NFL record. Even more stunning, the team went undefeated in the regular season, and was one *What the heck just happened?* play away from a perfect 19-0 record.

In the season-opener, New England ran the New York Jets off the field in a 38–14 rout, highlighted by Randy Moss's 51-yard touchdown and 183 receiving yards on 9 catches. Then the Patriots beat San Diego, prevailing by a 38–14 count for the second straight week, and then remarkably, put up 38 points for a third consecutive game, shredding Buffalo in the process, 38–7. New England soon became a juggernaut, bulldozing its competition. They were 5-0 before they scored 48 points in Dallas, and then a resounding 49 in Miami—Brady threw a team-record 6 touchdown passes in the game—and then 52 against Washington in a ruthless 45-point victory that left some critics assailing coach Belichick for running up the score.

Tom Brady led the charge on a Patriots' offensive attack that scored 75 touchdowns in 2007.
AP PHOTO / WINSLOW TOWNSON

New England was 8-0 and had outscored its opponents by a combined 204 points, 331 to 127. The closest score was 34–17 over Cleveland. Brady already had thrown 30 touchdown passes (he'd never thrown more than 28 in a season) against 2 interceptions. The touchdown record for a complete season was Peyton Manning's 49, set in 2004. Always the team man, Brady was not thinking about himself. "They're always meaningful games when you play them, and 8-0 is great," he said. "But it really doesn't guarantee us anything." Especially with the next game against Manning and the defending Super Bowl champion Colts.

Indianapolis had won 12 in a row, including beating the Pats for the AFC title nine months earlier. This game was close, and Brady even was intercepted twice.

But he threw 3 touchdown passes—2 in the fourth quarter—to overcome a 10-point deficit, in a 24–20 comeback win. "We knew there would be close games, and it means a lot to win one," Brady said. The team would need to win a few more that way, too.

New England came back from its bye week to rout Buffalo, 56–10, to move to 10-0 and drive the conversation about a perfect season into high gear. Back-to-back 3-point victories over Philadelphia and Baltimore preserved the streak. The win over the Ravens was highlighted by Brady's 8-yard touchdown pass to Jabar Gaffney with just fifty-five seconds left in the game.

In Week 14, the 9-3 Steelers were set to face the 12-0 Pats when Pittsburgh safety Anthony Smith guaranteed a Steelers victory. Belichick read

Tom Brady was called "the golden boy" in 2007, a season in which he threw a record 50 touchdown passes.
AP PHOTO / GREG TROTT

the safety's words to his team, and the Patriots responded as the Patriots often did. "*Well done* is always better than *well said*—that's been the motto of this team," Brady warned. Enraged by Smith's arrogance, Brady carved through the Pittsburgh defense like a surgeon with the ball in his hand, throwing for 399 yards and 4 touchdowns, removing any doubt as to which team was dominant. The Patriots won, 34–13, to go 13-0. All those "maybe they can go 16-0" musings grew louder. Another triumph over the Jets, and then a victory over Miami for 15-0 set up the ultimate regular-season game. "It would be a great thing to do, but it's not our main goal," Brady said of going 16-0. "What we are after is the Super Bowl."

Don Shula's 1972 Miami Dolphins were the only undefeated Super Bowl winners, but NFL teams were playing 14-game regular seasons back then. New England had a legitimate chance to become the league's first 16-0 regular-season team and its first 19-0 champ. That meant New England had a shot to become the greatest NFL team of all time. To complete the Patriots' undefeated season against the New York Giants in Giants Stadium, where Belichick had made a name for himself by winning his first two Super Bowl rings as defensive coordinator for Bill Parcells, would be perfect.

"THE GOLDEN BOY"

Tom Brady was having a magical season. He had thrown 48 touchdown passes in the first 15 games. Two more touchdowns in the final game against New York and he would break the all-time single-season record, which was held by Peyton Manning, who'd had 49 in 2004. Antonio Pierce, the Giants middle linebacker, had created headlines that week by saying that Brady was walking around "like he's Prince Charles, like he's the golden boy," and complaining that Brady seemed indignant anytime a defensive player managed to lay hands on him. Pierce certainly didn't want Brady setting a record against the Giants, led by quarterback Eli Manning, Peyton's little brother. "There might have been a little bit of an incentive for us to try and stop Tom Brady from getting that record," Pierce acknowledged.

The Patriots already had the number-one seed in the AFC wrapped up, and the Giants had secured a wild-card spot in the NFC. In other years, this game would have had all the ingredients for a meaningless three hours with the goal to rest the starters and make sure nobody picked up any new injuries going into the playoffs. Instead, the Giants promised they would use their starters and push the Patriots to the limit. Did they ever.

The Giants played inspired ball and were giving the Patriots a huge scare, as they held a 28–16 lead early in the third quarter, and 28–23 going into the fourth. Brady had only thrown 1 touchdown pass, to Moss, giving the Giants hope that he would at least end the season with only a share of the record. It was a lot to ask. Brady came into the game averaging more than 3 touchdown passes per game. By the fourth quarter, it became clear the Giants defense could no longer contain him; he was operating the highest-scoring offense in NFL history.

Early in the fourth quarter, Brady and Moss connected on a 65-yard touchdown score that set two records: Brady beat Manning's mark with his 50th touchdown pass, and Moss broke Jerry Rice's single-season record of 22 TD receptions. (Six years later, playing for the Broncos, Manning took back the record, with 55.) The Patriots rallied for a 38–35 win, and finished the regular season with an unblemished schedule. "In this game of football, it's hard to go 16-and-0," Moss said. "As a football player and a fan of the game, my hat's off to this organization."

New England had a shot to become the greatest NFL team of all time.

And hats off to Tom Terrific, who not surprisingly added NFL Most Valuable Player honors and Associated Press Male Athlete of the Year to the greatest season any quarterback ever had. Brady completed nearly 70 percent of his passes for 4,806 yards. Even more stunning, he attained those 50 touchdown passes against just 8 interceptions, and posted an amazing 117.2 passer rating, a mark that ranks among the highest in history. Moss had become the game's most dangerous receiver, catching 98 passes for 1,493 yards and an NFL-record 23 touchdowns. He became arguably the greatest deep threat in the history of the league, regularly catching passes in double and triple teams. The presence of Moss helped the slot receiver Wes Welker blossom in an incredible breakout season to catch 112 passes for 1,175 yards and 8 touchdowns. Welker probably fit his role in the Patriots' offense better than any one player ever has.

The 2007 Patriots left a memorable and historic imprint on the game. As a team, they set scoring records, with 75 touchdowns and 589 points. (Those same Manning-led Broncos surpassed the Pats' marks, with 76 TDs and 606 points in 2013.) New England's high-rolling, high-octane scoring machine torched its opponents, week after week, lighting up NFL stadium scoreboards like no team ever had before. Brady led the charge of a potent offensive attack that topped 50 points twice, 40 points four times, and 30 points twelve times. These numbers have value in meaning, but also in execution. Most important, New England won all 16 games on its schedule.

THRILLING REMATCH

As quarterback of the Patriots, Brady was responsible for having set numerous regular-season records and career highs for himself, his teammates, and the organization. Now he desired another Super Bowl ring. He displayed remarkable accuracy in the divisional playoff game against the Jacksonville Jaguars; only drops by Welker and Ben Watson prevented Brady from throwing a perfect game. He completed 26 of 28 passes for 262 yards and 3 touchdowns. "Those guys, when they are open like that, it's my job to hit them," Brady said. "It's easy when you have receivers that are open all the time and an offensive line that never lets anyone touch you. It makes it fun to play."

Brady did not fare as well statistically in the AFC Championship Game against the San Diego Chargers, throwing for 209 yards, 2 touchdowns, and 3 interceptions. Despite a shaky Brady—he injured his right ankle in the 21–12 victory—

"[Brady] has my vote for the greatest to ever lace them up in a quarterback position."

—RANDY MOSS,
HALL OF FAME WR

the Patriots won their eighteenth game of the season and advanced to the Super Bowl for the fourth time in seven years. The victory was also a milestone for Brady, the 100th win of his career, a feat accomplished in just 126 games, a record 16 games better than Joe Montana's ledger.

The New England Patriots arrived for Super Bowl XLII, played at University of Phoenix Stadium, in Glendale, Arizona, as the team receiving top billing, and according to many experts, hailed as the greatest team ever. Because the Patriots were undefeated, in pursuit of the mythic 19-0 season, and owners of the most prolific aerial circus in NFL history, while their opponent, the New York

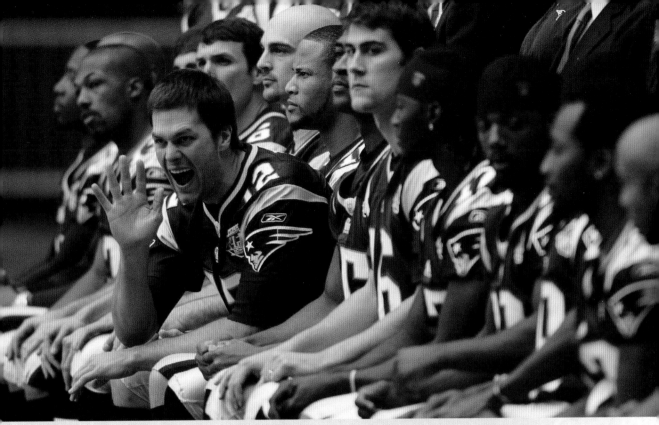

Tom Brady with the 2007 Patriots, the New England team he considers the best to ever take the field.
AP PHOTO / STEPHAN SAVOIA

Giants, had barely earned a playoff spot by squeaking through the NFC title game (largely because of a Brett Favre interception), the Giants seemed to be just another minor hurdle for the New Englanders to overcome.

Leading up to Super Sunday, almost every midweek story in the media included an angle about how the mighty Patriots had become a football powerhouse, the NFL's big bad bully, and the Giants were the puny kids on the beach, sure to have sand kicked in their face masks. Forgotten in all the hype and hoopla was the fact that this Super Bowl was also a rematch of the final game of the regular season, won by New England, 38–35. Despite the tough loss, the Giants believed they could beat the Pats. After all, they had come up just a field goal short against the best team in history.

The players competing in Super Bowl XLII really flipped the script on the sportswriters. While the offenses received the headlines, it was the defenses that

MAN DOWN

Tom Brady and the Patriots enjoyed a nearly perfect season in 2007, mesmerizing fans in every way imaginable. Brady's superhuman season earned him his first NFL Most Valuable Player award. Such an honor would have been a hallmark achievement, had the shocking Super Bowl loss not left such a sour taste. Now it was time for revenge. But just as everything was ruined in an instant at the end of Brady's last season, the same went for the beginning of the next one. In the Patriots' 2008 season-opener against Kansas City, Chiefs safety Bernard Pollard hit Brady low during the first quarter of the Patriots' 17–10 win at Gillette Stadium. Brady suffered torn anterior cruciate and medial collateral ligaments in his left knee, effectively ending his comeback before it began.

On the Patriots' 15th offensive snap of the game, Brady, who had completed 6 of his first 10 passes, dropped back to pass on first and 10 from the Kansas City 42-yard line. Pollard blitzed, but was picked up and blocked to the ground by Patriots running back Sammy Morris. As Brady stepped into what would be his 11th and final pass of the season—a 28-yard completion to Randy Moss—Pollard made a desperation dive at Brady's legs, his shoulder and helmet clipping the quarterback's left knee. Brady screamed, fell to the ground, and immediately clutched his knee to his chest. He lay on the turf as the Patriots' medical staff examined the injured leg. Brady limped off the field with help from team trainers, and headed directly to the locker room, with 7:27 remaining in the first quarter.

The hit appeared accidental and was not flagged by the officials. "Oh, man, I felt horrible," Pollard said. "Obviously, I heard everything when it popped. I felt it. I went to the sideline and the first thing I [thought] was, 'Hey, he's done.' I didn't mean to do that. Man, I was kind of freaking out. As a player, we don't want to see that. It was a crazy play." Pollard indirectly sent get-well wishes to the quarterback but never apologized. "There was no reason to apologize," Pollard said. "I didn't do anything wrong."

Brady never felt anger toward Pollard or bitterness over his first major injury. "It's football," he said. "There's no way he owes me an explanation." But he did admit to feeling "pretty empty" as he was being helped to the sideline. "You go down, they take you off the field, the ref blows the whistle, the 25-second clock starts, and they play the game without you," said Brady, who had made 127 consecutive starts. "You're like, 'Wow. That's really what it's like. They play without you.' "

A catastrophic knee injury caused Tom Brady to miss all but 15 snaps of the 2008 season. AP PHOTO / WINSLOW TOWNSON

With Brady out for the season, backup quarterback Matt Cassel became the starter and nearly led New England to the playoffs. Brady helped guide him through the season, sending him texts the night before each game and the morning after. While the injury was bad, the recovery was even worse, as Brady suffered an infection that required multiple surgeries. He had four surgeries in total, but was able to recover in time for the start of the 2009 season, which ended with another Pro Bowl selection and the Comeback Player of the Year award. The Patriots completed a 10-6 season with a humiliating (by their standards) home playoff loss to the Baltimore Ravens. It was New England's first home playoff loss in 9 games, with Brady under center.

Tom and Gisele married ten days after he popped the question, in 2009. Flashbulbs popped when the couple arrived for the Met Gala in 2017. PHOTO BY EVAN AGOSTINI / INVISION / AP

reigned supreme for forty-five minutes; the score was a meager 7–3 in favor of the Patriots entering the fourth quarter. On the Giants' first drive of the final period, quarterback Eli Manning tossed a scoring pass to seldom-used receiver David Tyree, putting the Giants ahead, 10–7, with eleven minutes left to play. The teams traded possessions over the next eight and a half minutes. New York's defensive line, led by Michael Strahan and Justin Tuck, harassed Brady all night, sacking him 5 times for losses totaling negative 37 yards. However, as advertised, Brady finally did respond with a touchdown march of his own, putting the Pats ahead with a 6-yard scoring strike to Moss.

Manning and the Giants got the ball back for a final drive. Down 14–10 with 1:16 left in Super Bowl XLII, New York faced a third-and-five on its own 44-yard line. On that play, Manning escaped several New England defenders and threw up a desperation heave to Tyree. In a jump ball against safety Rodney Harrison, Tyree caught the football by pinning it against his helmet, securing a 32-yard gain. It was a miracle catch. Said Tyree: "When I look at it, I don't think that's really something that's humanly possible. I couldn't work hard to do that. I couldn't train. It was like I was kind of the co-star and God was the star in that event." Four plays later, Manning lofted a pass to the left corner of the end zone. After shaking free from his man, wide receiver Plaxico Burress cradled the ball for a touchdown, and New York won the seesaw battle, 17–14, spoiling the Patriots' bid for an undefeated season. Aside from Joe Namath's guarantee in Super Bowl III, it was probably the biggest upset in Super Bowl history.

After winning three different Super Bowls by 3 points, New England finally lost one by the same margin. The disappointment in the New England locker room was palpable. The 2007 Patriots had made eighteen consecutive trips into postgame locker rooms, laughing and joking and reveling in their own glory, and suddenly the New England players were walking into a mausoleum. The Patriots were one minute away from beating the Giants—only to be robbed of the opportunity, thanks, in part, to Tyree's helmet catch. It was a soul-crushing defeat. "I probably need some time to reflect on the game and some time to reflect on the season," said Brady,

Few athletes transcend sports and become pop culture icons, but Brady is one of them.

who completed 29 of 48 passes for 266 yards, but was continuously harried by the Giants' defense. "It is extremely disappointing. This isn't something any of us prepared for."

An athlete in the prime of his career normally does not reminisce and reflect on past experiences—win or lose. However, when the time does arrive, and Brady looks back on his extraordinary career, his one major regret is likely to be not winning the Super Bowl with the marvelous 2007 team. "To me, that was the greatest team that ever played in the NFL," he said. "We won so many games against the toughest competition that year, by big margins."

MODEL RELATIONSHIP

Having suffered a traumatic knee injury, and enduring the painful and strenuous rehabilitation program that followed, Tom Brady leaned on his beautiful girlfriend for support. After dating for a little over two years, he and Gisele Bündchen were ready to take their relationship to the next level. In January, Brady proposed to Bündchen by tricking her into thinking her apartment was flooded, and so she rushed home to find a romantic scene set with candles and rose petals. "He went down on his knee to propose and I'm like, 'Get up!' because he just had surgery and had three staph infections," she told *Vogue*. "And I was like, 'What are you doing?' He's like, 'I gotta go on my knees,' and I'm like, 'No, no, no! Get up, please!'" The couple married on February 26, 2009, in a private ceremony in Santa Monica, California, and held a second ceremony on April 4 on the beach of Santa Teresa, Costa Rica, where they own a home.

Tom Brady now *was* the golden boy, his rakish smile beaming from the covers of urbane magazines that celebrate what it means to be a man in contemporary American culture. *Esquire* tagged him Best Dressed Man. *Details* labeled him Best of the Best Dressed Men. *GQ* dubbed him one of the 25 Coolest Athletes of All Time. Brady's unparalleled success on the field had turned him into an NFL legend, while his personal life and marriage to Gisele made them well suited as ideal fashion icons. The stylish pair regularly attends the annual gala at the Metropolitan Museum of Art in Manhattan to rave reviews on the red carpet.

Few athletes transcend sports and become pop culture idols, but Brady is one of them, making him the perfect pitchman for luxury products. He holds lucrative endorsement contracts with companies like TAG Heuer, Aston Martin, and Beats by Dre, just to name a few—elite brands that aim to sell to the guy in the luxury box. He has become a fixture modeling in print ads, which take advantage of his good looks, and establish the Patriots star as the embodiment of class, bolstering the perception that Brady-endorsed merchandise is a prestigious item. Bündchen also has made tons of money by allowing companies to monetize her

Paparazzi got the scoop on newlyweds Tom and Gisele while honeymooning in the bride's hometown of Horizontina, Brazil, on March 14, 2009. AP PHOTO / TADEU VILANI / AGENCIA RBS

name and likeness. With a net worth estimated at around $540 million, Brady and Bündchen are perennially named one of *Forbes'* World's Most Powerful Couples, right beside other dynamic duos such as Jay-Z and Beyoncé Knowles, and Victoria and David Beckham.

The year had been a wild roller-coaster ride for Brady, and it drew to a close at its highest point on December 8, 2009, when Gisele gave birth to the couple's first child, Benjamin Rein Brady. They had made the decision to have a water birth, and Gisele revealed that she delivered their son in the bathtub of their penthouse apartment in Boston. It was a special moment to cap off the year.

There was another special moment to cap off the decade, as the Associated Press honored Brady as the best pro football player of the first decade of the 2000s. It was an easy choice, for not only was Brady the most successful quarterback in the NFL, but his team was also at the top more than any other.

Tom Brady soared for the winning score in the AFC Championship Game and landed in his fifth Super Bowl. AP PHOTO / ELISE AMENDOLA

It is hard to remember a time when Tom Brady was not the face of football. And although he has taken his share of lumps over the past decade, the fire still burned hot within him at this time. He told *Sports Illustrated* in June 2009 that playing ten more seasons was "a big goal of mine, a very big goal. I want to play until I'm forty-one. And if I get to that point and still feel good, I'll keep playing. I mean, what else am I going to do? I don't like anything else.

"People say, 'What will you do if you don't play football?' Why would I even think of doing anything else? What would I do instead of running out in front of 80,000 people and command fifty-two guys I consider brothers and be one of the real gladiators? Why would I ever want to do anything else? It's so hard to think of anything that would match what I do. Fly to the moon? Jump out of planes? Bungee-jump off cliffs? None of that matters to me," he declared. "I want to play this game I love, be with my wife and son, and enjoy life."

NEW HEIGHTS

Like clockwork, Tom Brady barreled through opposing defenses in 2010, setting the tone for the rest of the league. He led the NFL with 36 touchdown passes (to just 4 interceptions), and helped the Patriots to a league-best 14-2 record, the fourth team in the Bill Belichick–Tom Brady era to win at least 14 games during the regular season. Though the Patriots suffered a crushing home playoff loss to Rex Ryan's New York Jets, Brady won his second Most Valuable Player award, becoming the first player to capture the award unanimously. The GOAT—Greatest of All Time—just kept collecting more bling.

Brady, thirty-three, proved to skeptics he was still Tom Terrific, and he also showed that the Brady brand was ready to reach new heights. In 2010, he ushered in a new era of endorsements, proving No. 12 is as shrewd a businessman as he is a quarterback. Brady left his sponsor, athletic-wear giant Nike, to sign with up-and-coming brand Under Armour. Under Armour had been rapidly growing since its inception in 1996, but Brady was by far the biggest name yet to represent the company. The savvy quarterback made an investment in it, taking stock in the company rather than cash. The deal has paid off handsomely. Brady's stock in Under Armour has made him millions, but his next sponsorship made him a fashion icon.

In arguably one of the boldest moves of his career, Brady ignored the skeptics and became the new face of the UGG for Men campaign. His deal with UGG was one that confused many, since the stylish sheepskin footwear—previously essential among hipsters and teenage girls—was not known as a men's brand at the time. A generous guy, Brady gave each of his teammates a pair of UGG slippers for Christmas, breaking down the wall for macho men to proudly traipse around in furry comfort. "We're probably the best-dressed offensive linemen in the NFL, thanks to Tom Brady," said Dan Connolly, a Pats guard from 2007 to 2014.

Even following an MVP season, Brady managed to outperform himself in 2011, passing for over 5,000 yards for the first time in his career. Brady threw for a career-high 517 yards and 4 touchdowns in a 38–24 victory over the Miami Dolphins in the season-opener. One score was a 99-yard touchdown pass to Wes Welker—a record-tying feat that can never be broken. "I only threw it 25 yards. Wes did all the work," said the appreciative signal caller. Led by the quarterback's golden right arm, the Patriots finished the season 13-3 and were rewarded with the home-field advantage throughout the playoffs.

Brady was laser-focused for the postseason. He honed in on his receivers to throw 6 touchdown passes in a 45–10 win against Denver in the division-round game, earning a share of the postseason record

> "People can hate on him, y'all can be mad at him, but he's the best quarterback we've ever seen."
>
> —RAY LEWIS,
> HALL OF FAME LB

first set by Oakland's Daryle ("The Mad Bomber") Lamonica, and then equaled by San Francisco's Steve Young. The victory over the Broncos also added up to Brady and coach Belichick earning sole possession of the NFL record for post-season wins by a quarterback-coach duo with 15, surpassing the 14 Pittsburgh's Chuck Noll and Terry Bradshaw won together.

In the AFC Championship Game, Brady failed to throw a touchdown pass for the first time in 36 games, though he scored the winning touchdown against the Baltimore Ravens by catapulting his body over the vaunted Baltimore defense, a 1-yard leap in the fourth quarter to seal a hard-fought victory. Brady absorbed a bone-rattling collision with the ferocious linebacker Ray Lewis, and then the quarterback emphatically spiked the ball as he walked away. The Patriots held tight for a satisfying 23–20 victory, sending Brady to his fifth Super Bowl, one more than Montana.

SUPER REMATCH

It looked like another fantastic season and a fairy-tale ending as the Patriots once again met Tom Coughlin's Giants in football's ultimate game. In this Super Bowl rematch, just three Patriots players who appeared in Super Bowl XLII remained—Brady, defensive tackle Vince Wilfork, and placekicker Stephen Gostkowski—and they'd had plenty of time to recover from that stinging defeat. "That was a long, long time ago," Gostkowski said. "Obviously, losing in the Super Bowl hurts. But as players, you've got to learn to move on from wins and losses."

This matchup between the Patriots and Giants in Super Bowl XLVI was eerily similar to the first Super Sunday meeting four years earlier. The Patriots had a death grip on the game—a 17–15 lead, and the ball—with a little more than four minutes to play. On second-and-11 from the Giants' 44-yard line, Brady spotted Wes Welker wide open downfield and, suddenly, as the ball spiraled through the air in Welker's direction, New England's fortunes to win a fourth title seemed certain. Welker possessed great hands. He posted career highs of 1,569 yards on 122 catches and 9 touchdowns during the regular season. He'd also caught all 7 passes Brady threw his way inside Lucas Oil Stadium. But the normally reliable Welker inexplicably dropped the ball, much to the chagrin of the Patriots defenders on the bench, who were shown on the NBC broadcast dropping their heads in disbelief and disappointment.

A closer look revealed that Brady's pass had sailed slightly high and behind Welker, who was able to get his hands on the ball but couldn't pull it in. Welker crumpled on the field near the New York 20, his head in his hands. On the ensuing drive, history repeated itself in incredible fashion as the Giants rode another heart-crushing fourth-quarter comeback by Eli Manning to win the championship, 21–17. Winning the Lombardi Trophy twice in five seasons against the same rivals—a team with three Super Bowl rings of its own—stands alone as an amazing achievement, but for the Giants to do it again by nearly duplicating their miraculous championship run from 2007, right down to the final, nerve-wracking drive, is astonishing.

> "I think Tom Brady is the greatest football player we've ever had."
> —MICHAEL STRAHAN, HALL OF FAME DEFENSIVE END

Ultimately, the Brady-to-Welker incompletion is remembered as the costliest missed opportunity of the game. Had quarterback and receiver made a connection, the Patriots would have been close to putting the game on ice with time winding down. Brady refused to pin the blame on Welker for the Patriots' loss. "You win as a team and you lose as a team, and certainly one play wasn't why we lost," said a stoic Brady, who completed 27 of 41 passes—including a record 16 in a row—for 276 yards, with 2 touchdowns and 1 interception. His counterpart Eli Manning was named Super Bowl MVP for the second time. "Certainly Eli has had a great season. He made some great throws in the fourth quarter, and they deserved to win," Brady said.

FAMILY TIES

Starting off 2012 with another heart-wrenching Super Bowl loss was rough, but there were good things to come off the field. In April, Brady's sister, Julie, married former Red Sox player and two-time World Series winner Kevin Youkilis. The wedding simply added to the royal Brady bloodline, as he now had another great Boston athlete as his brother-in-law. Youkilis, a three-time American League All-Star and a Gold Glove winner in 2007, was inducted into the Red Sox Hall of Fame in 2018. Not only did Brady's extended family grow with his sister's wedding, but his own brood grew as well. Gisele gave birth to Vivian Lake Brady in the comfort of the couple's Boston home on December 5, adding the first daughter to the ever-growing Brady bunch. "I grew up in a house with three sisters, so I think it's great for my boys to have a girl in the house, just to understand a little bit of what makes a woman tick," Brady told ESPN. "She's a beautiful little girl."

Brady continued playing at a Pro Bowl level in 2012, leading the Patriots to a 12-4 record. He finished the season with 4,827 passing yards, 34 touchdowns, only 8 interceptions, and a passer rating of 98.7. The Patriots scored 557 total points, the fifth highest in league history, and Brady became the first quarterback to lead his team to ten division titles. He was getting so good at this playoff thing that he seemed to be competing for a championship every year. Like déjà vu all over again, Brady and the Patriots earned yet another chance at Super Bowl glory after New England's 41–28 shellacking of the Houston Texans in the divisional round. With the victory, the seventeenth of Brady's postseason career, he had outdone his childhood hero, Joe Montana, and a fourth NFL championship would equal Montana's final haul. "I love playing, I love competing, I love being part of this organization," said Brady, who threw for 3 touchdowns and 344 yards. "I've just been fortunate to play on some great teams over the years. I never take it for granted."

Although it's true that Brady authored a strong playoff performance against Houston, he followed up that game with a disastrous second act against Baltimore in the AFC Championship Game, an uninspiring 28–13 loss. Brady, operating against an opportunistic Ravens secondary, showed uncharacteristically poor judgment by throwing two fourth-quarter interceptions. The Pats committed a third turnover by fumbling, and the team frittered away its 13–7 halftime lead. Brady had lost for the time ever in Foxborough after holding a halftime lead—he had been 67-0.

During the off-season, Brady and the Patriots agreed on a three-year contract extension, which would keep him with the team through 2017, when he'd be forty years old. What's noteworthy about the new contract was that he stood to collect just $27 million over the three years, which essentially was half of his market value. It was the second time in Brady's career that he had left a stack of money on the bargaining table in order to give the Patriots a competitive advantage.

Winning, of course, isn't the sole focus of Brady's life—at least not in the off-season. He also is very giving of his time to charitable causes. When Brady's sister, Nancy, went to Uganda on a public health fellowship to help some of the world's poorest children, the quarterback decided to buy laptops as part of the One Laptop Per Child effort in the African country. He committed to buying 1,500 laptops and sent them to his sister while she was doing a mission in Kampala, Uganda, with the Infectious Disease Institute. Nancy hand-delivered the personal computers to the youngsters. Brady wanted to help "carry out this wonderful charity's vision to give every child a chance to connect with the rest of the world no matter their personal circumstances." He has also donated thousands of laptops to be distributed to Boys and Girls Clubs in the New England area.

There are many various charities for which Brady helps to raise money, including the Dana-Farber Cancer Institute, in Boston. Over the years, at the annual fund-raiser, the quarterback has helped raise a total of more than $6.5 million for cancer research by shaving his head in a close buzz cut. And through Goodwill of Boston, Brady and his Patriots teammates have served food to the area homeless population on Thanksgiving Day. "Helping out is something I have always believed is important," he said. "I'm happy to do it, and happy to have the opportunity to do it."

CHAPTER 10
CAPTAIN MARVEL

TOM BRADY HAS BEEN A CRUNCH-TIME MAGICIAN SINCE COL-lege, but the Brady legend began to truly blossom when he led the New England Patriots to late game-winning drives in his first three Super Bowls. Quarterbacks like Brady are discussed in heroic terms mainly because they're able to pull out victories in pressure-packed situations where mere mortals would surely fail. He's the reason opponents don't want the Patriots to have final possession of the ball in a close game. Time and again, Brady has proven to be a mastermind in the clutch, demonstrating that he knows how to handle the big moment better than any other player in the league. When New England needs Brady to make a big play, far more often than not, that is exactly what he does.

The 2013 season would bring more of the same. The Pats again finished with a 12-4 record, and the thirty-six-year-old quarterback led the charge during three memorable comebacks for his team. The first came in Week 6 against the New Orleans Saints, when Brady drove the Pats 70 yards down the field before throwing the game-winning touchdown in the closing seconds for a 30–27 triumph. But nothing matched what he did in Week 12 versus the Denver Broncos, when the Patriots trailed 24–0 at halftime. Brady tossed three second-half touchdowns while leading the team on 6 total scoring drives. The Pats scored 31 unanswered points and then won in overtime. And as the Cleveland Browns discovered in Week 14, whenever future Hall of Famers Tom Brady and Bill Belichick are stalking the opposite side of the field, no lead is safe. Down 26–14 with 2:30 left,

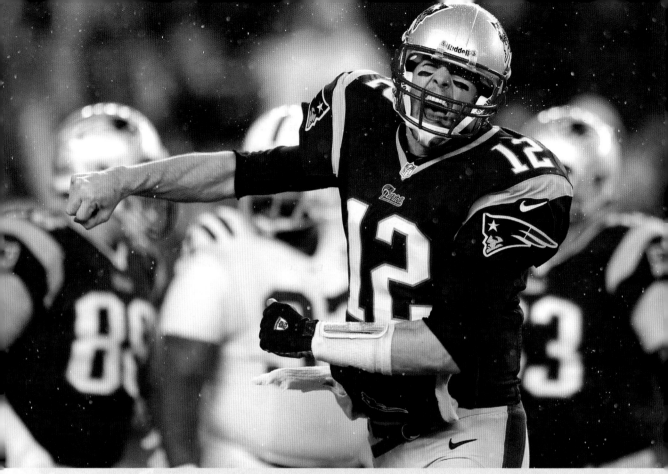

Tom Brady has proven to be a mastermind in the clutch, demonstrating that he knows how to handle the big moment better than any other player in the league. AP PHOTO / MICHAEL DWYER

Brady threw 2 touchdown passes in a thirty-second span—aided by the recovery of an onside kick—to win 27–26 in a wild, improbably thrilling finish.

The Brady magic never waned—at least, not until the AFC Championship Game, a disappointing 26–16 loss in Denver. Brady passed for 277 yards and 2 touchdowns (1 rushing), but it didn't really matter, because the Patriots had been stopped 1 game short of a Super Bowl appearance for a second straight year. While the season wasn't Brady's best—he spent a lot of time yelling at his teammates early in the season, and he couldn't even get a high five toward the end (creating a trending meme)—he still displayed the ability to make even the most unlikely receiver a late-game hero. He had thrown touchdown passes in a remarkable 52 consecutive games, an extraordinary run that ended in a 13–6

Week 5 loss at Cincinnati. Although his quest for NFL history was broken 2 games short of Drew Brees' record 54-game streak, Brady was unfazed at falling short of personal goals. He's made it clear he plays for one thing—victories. "I'm bummed that we lost," he said. "I think that's all that really matters."

The Patriots hadn't won a Super Bowl in nearly a decade, and although Brady hadn't been shy about stating his desire to play into his forties, his numbers (judging by his own high standards) had taken a nosedive, alarming those who wondered if the end was near. Most great quarterbacks have lost quite a bit by their late thirties, though there have been exceptions: Warren Moon tossed 25 touchdown passes in 1997, at age forty-one; Brett Favre was forty when he led the Vikings to the 2009 NFC title game; and Peyton Manning was thirty-seven when he threw an NFL-record 55 touchdown passes in 2013.

FORGET ABOUT THE FIRST HALF

Tom Brady and Peyton Manning played a number of classics over the years, but they never played a game quite like the one at Gillette Stadium on November 24, 2013, with the Pats overcoming a 24-point deficit on their home turf to win, 34–31.

Even before the game, headlines were blaring about the much-heralded matchup between Brady and Manning. The Sunday-night showdown was billed as a battle of two legendary quarterbacks, the fourteenth meeting between them, and it turned out to be one of the wildest games for both teams in recent memory.

The Broncos jumped out to a 24–0 lead in the first half following 3 Patriots turnovers. "You've got to forget about what happened in the first half, because it was a terrible half of football," said Brady, who connected on 21 of 26 attempts for 228 yards and 3 TDs following the intermission.

After New England came storming back in the second half and scored 31 unanswered points, Manning rallied the Broncos to tie the game. In overtime, a special teams fumble recovery by New England's punt coverage unit that resulted in Stephen Gostkowski's game-winning field goal was the difference.

"What a crazy game, and what a fun finish," Gostkowski said.

Tom Brady plays his best football when the game is on the line, as he did during a memorable comeback victory against the Denver Broncos in 2013.
AP PHOTO / ELISE AMENDOLA

For Brady, the writing seemed to be on the wall. The Patriots had just drafted a quarterback prospect from Eastern Illinois named Jimmy Garoppolo. Belichick announced that New England needed to address the quarterback situation for the future, and that he wanted to be "early rather than late at that position." In the face of uncertain circumstances, Brady gained motivation from the doubt, remembering it in the toughest times, and he used it as fuel moving forward. He wanted to prove people wrong, and his single-minded drive pushed him to reach new heights.

THE TB12 METHOD

Tom Brady was on a mission to silence his critics and alleviate all concerns that he might be washed up. For years and years, with his laser arm and focus, and his raging fire and computer-like football brain, he had been able to overcome Father Time. Although this was no longer the case for Brady, the great ones figure out ways to compensate once they recognize even the subtlest signs of slippage. Muhammad Ali knew he couldn't dance at age thirty-two against George Foreman as he had at age twenty-two against Sonny Liston; hence, the rope-a-dope. "With every level you reach, everyone gets faster, stronger, and better, and I had to work really hard just to be competitive," said Brady.

Realizing he'd need to be faster and more explosive if he wanted any shot of sticking around in the NFL—which for most players stands for Not For Long— the quarterback embarked on a grueling process that would begin to transform his body. In 2013 he hired a strength-and-conditioning coach, Alex Guerrero, and carved out secret daily workouts at six o'clock in the morning, when no one else was around. "I love what I do, and I want to do it for a long time," Brady said. "When you're one of the leaders of a team, there are no days off."

With the goal of reducing inflammation in the aging quarterback's body, Guerrero designed workouts to make Brady's muscles more pliable and less susceptible to injury. Brady does these workouts on dry land, on sand, and in water. He hardly ever lifts weights but works mainly with resistance bands, because the

BODY GURU

Tom Brady's ability to defy the cruel and inevitable process of aging is due, in large part, to his intense training regimen labeled as the TB12 Method, developed with the help of Alex Guerrero, a health guru who works with Brady at least once every day, and whose duties include spiritual guide, counselor, nutrition adviser, trainer, and massage therapist. Guerrero is a California native with a master's degree in traditional Chinese medicine. Teammates describe him as Brady's Mr. Miyagi. They say he knows the quarterback's body better than Gisele Bündchen, Brady's wife. "I do have my hands on him a little more than she does," Guerrero joked.

Guerrero is Brady's body coach and business partner—and godfather to Brady's youngest son, Ben—and he's one of the main reasons the quarterback hasn't missed a single start since blowing out his knee in 2008. As an athlete, Brady's chief asset is his availability to play. Advances in sports medicine, exercise performance data, and strength and flexibility training, along with smarter diets and lifestyle choices, have aided Brady's sustained assault on excellence. The implementation of rule changes further protecting quarterbacks certainly hasn't hurt, either. All of these factors help to promote Brady's status as an enduring symbol of the steroid-free athlete.

focus is on speed, agility, and core stability. As part of his strict personal regimen, Brady has adopted a specific game plan to help him stay at the top of his craft. Every day is micromanaged to a precise schedule: treatment, workouts, food, recovery, practice, rest. And those schedules aren't just for a week, or a month, or a season. They're for five years. When teammates ask how long the quarterback intends to play, he simply says, "Forever."

"You'll hear people say, 'Football doesn't define me,'" said Guerrero. But that's not Brady. "Football isn't what Tom does—football *is* Tom. This is who he is."

With guidance from his guru, Brady tries to be better through self-awareness (he meditates), rest and repair (he sleeps in special "athlete recovery sleepwear"), and nutrition (he won't eat dairy, caffeine, white sugar, or white flour). But Brady adds that he is not as militant about his diet and fitness routine as people may think. "If I'm craving bacon, I have a piece. Same with pizza," he told *Men's Health*. "You should never restrict what you really want. We're humans, here for one life." On his cheat day, if he's feeling a little crazy, he'll chow down on some avocado ice cream with cacao mixed in to mimic chocolate. "Tastes great," Brady claims, not all that convincingly.

Brady eats a mostly organic, local, and plant-based diet with no highly processed foods, and spikes all his water (purified only, please) with electrolytes. Brady claims to drink between fourteen and thirty-seven glasses of water per day, which at eight-ounces per glass, is enough water to hydrate a healthy person for several days. "Drink at least one-half of your body weight in ounces of water every day. That's the minimum," he advises in his book, *The TB12 Method: How to Achieve a Lifetime of Sustained Peak Performance*, which reached No. 1 on the *New York Times* bestseller list, and topped Amazon's list within forty-eight hours of its release.

The dynamic workouts and new-age training methods have proven to be a game-changer for Brady, who isn't aging as much as he is evolving. At the beginning of each season, the Patriots run their players through a battery of strength, speed, and agility testing similar to combine drills. The purpose is to measure how the players are declining. But the damnedest thing happened with Brady after beginning his new regimen in 2013. According to Guerrero, he improved his test scores in every category. "It seems he's actually gotten stronger and faster as he's gotten older," he said.

Tom Brady proves that age is just a state of mind.

Justin Edelman, who became Brady's teammate in 2009, believes the quarterback is an ageless wonder. "It's unbelievable to see a thirty-nine-year-old man play like he's twenty-nine," said Edelman, in 2016. "His body hasn't really changed. He may have lost some hair. Other than that, he's still the same."

Tom Brady turned thirty-seven before the start of the 2014 season, and he looked a little creaky in the first three games, winning two but failing to crack

Tom Brady works diligently with a strength and conditioning coach to improve his speed and explosiveness.
AP PHOTO / MICHAEL DWYER

250 passing yards in any. Then came the Week 4 debacle, a *Monday Night Football* game played against the Kansas City Chiefs, for all to see. Brady threw for a meager 159 yards with 2 interceptions and a strip-sack, resulting in a lost fumble returned for a touchdown. The second interception was a brutal pick-six that gave Kansas City a 41–7 lead early in the fourth quarter. Belichick had seen enough, and he benched Brady in favor of Garoppolo.

The Patriots were blown out of the water, 41–14, with many pegging New England as "done" after starting the season 2-2. The *Boston Globe* published an article titled "End Game Becomes Apparent," declaring it was time "to start wondering if the clock is running out on Brady's Patriots tenure a lot more quickly than we thought." Following the loss, coach Belichick gave one of his most

Belichickian news conferences of all time. He responded to reporters' questions by saying, "We're on to Cincinnati," five times, letting everyone know that he had moved on from the loss to the Chiefs.

Suddenly, the Sunday-night home game against the Bengals had become a referendum on whether Brady's days were numbered in New England. He responded with a vintage performance—a season-high 292 passing yards (becoming the sixth NFL quarterback to surpass 50,000 career yards) and 2 touchdowns in a 43–17 victory that felt just as profound as New England's 41–14 defeat in Kansas City.

Prognosticating Brady's demise has been a football sideshow for the better part of a decade. For just as long, Brady has proven the doubters wrong. The Patriots went on from Cincinnati and forged a 7-game winning streak, during which Brady threw 22 touchdown passes, to cap a strong finish to the season. In 2014, he threw for 4,109 yards and 33 touchdowns with what one might fairly describe as the least intimidating set of wide receivers he's ever had. Thanks to a strong stretch run, New England finished the season with a 12-4 record (again) and earned a twelfth AFC East title in thirteen seasons, with a healthy Brady under center.

LIGHTNING ROD

Adoption of the new-age TB12 Method had Brady positioned to make another run at the Lombardi Trophy, which had eluded him and the Patriots since 2005. Getting past Baltimore in the divisional round required one big comeback—and then another. Brady dug the Patriots out of two 14-point holes—the first team to do that in NFL playoff history—to bury the Ravens in a spine-tingling back-and-forth contest that captivated football fans from start to finish.

In an absolute classic, Brady's third touchdown pass of the game gave New England its first lead late in the fourth quarter. The quarterback led a masterful 74-yard march, and then hit Brandon LaFell for a 23-yard touchdown pass, with 5:13 left for the game-winner. It was a thrilling game of shifting momentum—2

Tom Brady leading the charge as the Patriots take the field for Super Bowl XLIX against the Seattle Seahawks.
AP PHOTO / DAVID J. PHILLIP

touchdowns by the Ravens, the next 2 by the Patriots, 2 more by the Ravens, and another 2 by the Patriots. "Behind twice by 14 wasn't necessarily in the plan," said Brady, who completed 8 of 9 passes for 72 yards on the winning drive. "It took a lot of execution to overcome it."

The quarterback who didn't get rattled and, ultimately, didn't fold, had to operate without anything resembling a running game (14 yards, the second fewest in team postseason history). Brady went 33-for-50 for 367 yards, with 3 touchdowns, and also ran for a score. He put the entire team on his back and came away with his 19th career playoff win, and it was one for the annals. He passed

Joe Montana for the most postseason touchdown passes in NFL history, with 46. He moved past Peyton Manning into the lead for most career postseason passing yards. He matched Montana's NFL-record five career postseason fourth-quarter comebacks. And now he was 1 game away from his sixth Super Bowl appearance.

The seesaw victory over Baltimore catapulted New England toward the AFC Championship Game for a fourth straight year. In the title game, the Patriots dismantled the Indianapolis Colts, 45–7, before a raucous, rain-soaked crowd in Foxborough; it was the second-most lopsided AFC championship victory ever. Scoring touchdowns on its first four second-half possessions, the Patriots earned the right to face the defending champion Seattle Seahawks for the NFL title, where Belichick would face Pete Carroll, whom he replaced as Patriots coach in 2000. "I only have one thing to say. We're on to Seattle," Belichick said, echoing the statement ("We're on to Cincinnati") he'd repeated several times after the 41–14 loss at Kansas City had dropped the Patriots to 2-2.

> "The thing about Tom is he's super clutch. He's on time. When the game's on the line, he has no fear."
> —RUSSELL WILSON, PRO BOWL QB

Football fans who appreciate greatness appreciate Tom Brady, and all that he stands for. Year in, year out, he is the most consistent quarterback in the sport. When he is under center in a game, the Patriots can never be counted out. He's that good. "Tom Brady is so special because he's such a great leader, and all the players can relate to him," said owner Robert Kraft.

Indeed, Brady has earned the respect of his teammates, and when he speaks up, they all listen. Deion Branch, who won the Super Bowl XXXIX Most Valuable Player award as a result of being on the receiving end of 11 Brady passes for 133 yards, may have summed up Brady best: "Tom thinks he's one of the boys. He can't be one of the boys. This guy is the face of the NFL."

Brady is beloved in Boston and is a civic treasure, along with Bill Russell, Larry Bird, Bobby Orr, Carl Yastrzemski, and David Ortiz. He has become celebrated for his ability to stand out at the top of his profession while maintaining a genuine connection with other people. There is something about him that is real.

"HE IS CAPTAIN AMERICA"

The Super Bowl XLIX matchup between the Patriots and Seattle Seahawks, played at the University of Phoenix Stadium, in Glendale, Arizona, was dubbed "The Duel in the Desert." A dry spell of three years had passed since New England's last trip to the championship game—a ten-year drought since the Patriots' last win on Super Sunday.

The Seahawks were a hot team. Winners of nine of the final ten regular-season games and the defending champs, and led by an impenetrable defense known as the Legion of Boom, they were thirsty for more.

New England trailed the Seahawks by 10 points, 24–14, in the fourth quarter, and was basically lacking a running game, rushing 21 times for 57 yards. So the Patriots were going to have to throw the ball the length of the field against one of the most vaunted defenses in the annals of the NFL. Seattle finished the regular season with the league's best defense in points, total yards, and passing yards allowed.

History was not on the side of the Pats. To this point, twenty-nine teams had held a 10-point second-half lead in the Super Bowl, and no team had ever lost. None, however, had to stop Tom Brady. He already shared the record for most postseason comebacks (five, with Joe Montana) and owned the record for post-season game-winning drives (eight). On this day, the thirty-seven-year-old was more than up to the challenge. In a fourth quarter that will be remembered for a long time, Brady completed 13 of 15 passes for 124 yards and 2 touchdowns. After his final throw of the night—a 3-yard touch-down pass to Julian Edelman, with 2:06 remaining—New England had taken a 28–24 lead.

Following a decade-long drought, Tom Brady's Patriots were champions again.

Super Bowl XLIX was far from over, though. The Patriots had to hang on at the end. Seven years ago on the same turf in Glendale, Giants receiver David Tyree had made the improb-able helmet catch that set the stage for a heartbreaking 17–14 defeat in Super Bowl XLII, ending an undefeated season. On this night, it was Seahawks receiver

Tom Brady and the Patriots were flying high against the Seattle Seahawks in the second half of Super Bowl XLIX.
AP PHOTO / DAVID GOLDMAN

Jermaine Kearse making an equally improbable juggling catch while on his back-side for a 33-yard gain, putting Seattle 5 yards away from breaking the Patriots' hearts again. "How many more plays are the Patriots going to have like this?" asked NBC's Cris Collinsworth after the first-down play. "David Tyree, Mario Manningham, and now, Kearse."

Seattle suddenly was in prime position to score the go-ahead touchdown—even more so after Marshawn Lynch gained 4 yards on the very next play, barely stopped short of the end zone by Dont'a Hightower. On second down, Seattle coach Pete Carroll surprised everyone by calling a pass play instead of a hand-off to Lynch, who had 102 yards on 24 carries in the game. Cornerback Malcolm Butler, an undrafted rookie, broke on a quick slant, his daring dash beating receiver Ricardo Lockett to the spot on the goal line. The two collided as Butler made the game-clinching interception.

The Pats' Super Bowl win was a thriller for the ages. Butler's play was the headliner—no Super Bowl game had ever swung so wildly on a single play—but, make no mistake, it was Brady's heroics that won this game, and the fourth Super Bowl title in fourteen years for the Patriots. "He's like playing against Bobby Fischer in chess," said Seattle's Michael Bennett. "It's just hard to beat him. He is Captain America."

Brady and Belichick embraced after beating the Seahawks in one of the best Super Bowls of all time. "Way to go, man. That's tremendous. Great job," an emotional Belichick told Brady, who responded with "What a win, huh?" and a huge smile.

Brady was the Super Bowl MVP for a third time. He completed 37 of 50 passes for 328 yards, with 4 touchdown passes, each to a different receiver, including an 8-for-8 run of perfection on the final drive that led to the go-ahead score with about two minutes left in the game. It is an ability to control and compartmentalize the noise—much like he does his nerves—in an urgent fourth-quarter comeback, that

"We're in the locker room with a walking legend. Tom has the most wins in quarterback history in the NFL, but he still comes to work like he hasn't accomplished anything."
—MALCOLM BUTLER, PRO BOWL CORNERBACK

may be Brady's most otherworldly gift. "Well, it's been a long journey," sighed a resolute Brady on the field after a tough game. "I've been at it for fifteen years and we've had a couple of tough losses in this game. This one came down to the end, and this time, we made the plays."

In the days leading up to Super Bowl XLIX against Seattle, Brady grew nostalgic, using the occasion of Throwback Thursday to upload a photograph of himself as a kid, posing in a replica Montana jersey. Then Brady did a fairly good impression of Joe Cool against Seattle, and surpassed his idol as the most prolific touchdown maker in Super Bowl history. "I haven't thought about that; I never put myself in those discussions," said Brady, when asked about his place

Tom Brady's heroics in the fourth quarter pointed the way to a Patriots' win in Super Bowl XLIX.
AP PHOTO / DAVID J. PHILLIP

alongside Montana, considered the greatest clutch quarterback in NFL history. "That's not how I think. There [are] so many great players that have been on so many great teams, and we've had some great teams that haven't won it, and I think you've just got to enjoy the moment."

STILL STANDING

The mood at Gillette Stadium was festive for the 2015 home-opener. Before kickoff, the Patriots unveiled their fourth championship banner as owner Robert Kraft and three former players—Troy Brown, Willie McGinest, and Ty

Law—carried out the most coveted prizes in the trophy case: New England's four Lombardis. Brady, the three-time Super Bowl MVP, was in midseason—or should we say postseason?—form, throwing 4 touchdown passes and setting a team record with 19 straight completions in a 28–21 win over the Pittsburgh Steelers. "It was a pretty special night," said Brady, whose 161 victories with one franchise as a starting quarterback had set an NFL record.

Three of Brady's four scoring strikes were thrown to a new favorite target, Rob Gronkowski. The Patriots' twenty-six-year-old tight end, known simply as Gronk, is that rarest of athletes, a physical freak in a league of physical freaks, so talented that even his fellow players, who are among the finest athletes in the country, can't believe what they are seeing. At 6-foot-6, Gronk stands 1 inch taller than three-time NFL Defensive Player of the Year J. J. Watt. At 264 pounds, he weighs 14 pounds more than four-time NBA champion LeBron James. And at 4.68 seconds, his 40-yard dash time was just 0.03 seconds slower than the time Heisman Trophy winner Tim Tebow ran at the same NFL Combine the Gronk attended, in 2010. "For a guy to be that big, that fast, that strong, it's really . . . it's not right," Patriots backup quarterback Jimmy Garoppolo said.

Brady's season got off to a fast start, and Gronkowski did what Gronkowski did best, which was delivering key blocks and beating tight coverages. Through 10 games Brady had thrown for 3,320 yards, a league-best 25 TDs, and just 4 picks. And he found Gronk with bodies draped all over him for 51 catches, 8 touchdowns, and 5 100-yard receiving games, during the same stretch. Naturally, the Patriots erupted to a blistering 10–0 start. Following a 36–7 Week 8 victory over Miami, in which he threw for 356 yards and 4 touchdowns, Brady was honored as the AFC Offensive Player of the Week—for the twenty-fifth time in his career.

Brady, thirty-eight, was destroying the NFL with the best form of his life. He passed for 4,770 yards and an NFL-high 36 touchdowns, against just 7 interceptions. He was spreading the ball around to a nearly unparalleled degree, with 10 different receivers making at least 10 catches—a main factor that is indicative not only of the team's success, but also of the weight on the quarterback's shoulders. He also completed a career-high 402 passes, yet still pounded the ground in frustration over a single missed third-down pass. His wife told Robert Kraft that she woke up at 3:30 in the morning to find her husband studying film. "Other than playing football, the other thing I love to do is preparing to play football," said Brady. "Football to me is more than just a sport. It has become my life."

By season's end, the Pats would finish with a won-loss record of—wait for it!—12-4, for a fourth straight season, to add another division title to New England's vast collection of banners. In the postseason, Brady hit Gronk with 2 touchdown passes and reached over the goal line for another score, as he led the Pats into the AFC title game for the fifth year in a row, with a 27–10 win over the Chiefs.

"I played for the Indianapolis Colts . . . with Peyton Manning. It's hard for me to say this, but it's true: Tom Brady is the best of all time."
—REGGIE WAYNE, PRO BOWL WR

Brady played in the conference title game for the tenth time in his career in Denver, a mile high, against Peyton Manning and the Broncos. Brady completed 27 of 56 attempts for 310 yards and a touchdown, but he threw 2 interceptions and got pummeled by the Broncos' defense. New England lost the game, 20–18, after a potential game-tying 2-point conversion attempt failed with seventeen seconds left in regulation. Belichick called the defeat in Denver a "crash landing" after Brady absorbed 20 hits and 4 sacks, and after Stephen Gostkowski missed his first extra-point kick in nine years and 524 attempts. The Patriots were manhandled, and yet, in a testament to Brady's resourcefulness, he somehow gave his team a chance to tie Denver in the final seconds. It was the final meeting between two storied quarterbacks; forty-three days later, Manning retired.

The granite-jawed Brady is chiseled on the NFL Quarterback's Mount Rushmore of the Super Bowl era, and a strong case can be made for him as the greatest to ever play the position. He is the ultimate technician, and obsesses over his well-grooved throwing motion to the point of vanity. (He won't autograph a

BRADY VS. MANNING

For fifteen years, Tom Brady and Peyton Manning were the NFL's answer to Magic vs. Bird, Chamberlain vs. Russell, Ali vs. Frazier, Palmer vs. Nicklaus, and Nadal vs. Federer. Elite players battling for championships. The preeminent quarterbacks of their generation went head to head seventeen times. (Bart Starr and Johnny Unitas met sixteen times, but they played in the same conference back when the NFL had only fourteen teams.)

Brady won 11 of the 17 matchups for a .647 winning percentage. He reeled off the first 6 games and then Manning won 3, culminating with the pulse-pounding 38–34 victory in the 2006 title game, the tilt that forever changed our perception of the rivalry. Brady went on to win 4 of the next 5, and then Manning won 2 of the last 3. The pair squared off 5 times in the postseason. That is the most of any two quarterbacks in NFL history. Four times they faced off in conference title games.

"It's been a great honor and privilege to have competed against him so many times," said Manning of his nemesis. "I have great respect for the way he takes care of himself physically and always answers the bell." Although Manning has a 3-1 edge over Brady in games with a trip to the Super Bowl on the line, Brady has the edge where it matters most: championship rings and career wins.

Tom Brady usually got the better of Peyton Manning in their head-to-head matchups, but not in the AFC title game following the 2015 season. AP PHOTO / DAVID ZALUBOWSKI

photo if he doesn't like the looks of his throwing mechanics.) He also has a taste for tedium, like planning workout routines months in advance, and he savors the minute details that keep him in the present instead of worrying about consequences, whether it be the outcome of a league title game or his place among the greatest quarterbacks in NFL history.

Of all the marvels of Brady's exceptional career, the most impressive might just be the dominant fashion in which he has reimagined what is possible for aging athletes. Stiff-arming Father Time, Brady managed to increase his efficiency across the board in completion percentage, yards per attempt, yards per game, touchdown-to-interception ratio, and passer rating, every year from ages thirty-six to thirty-nine. Beyond the numbers, No. 12 has also mastered situational football, spreading the ball around, controlling tempo, attacking the right matchup on the right down and distance, and turning the two-minute drill into a science. In December 2019, to commemorate the league's one hundredth anniversary, the NFL unveiled the ten quarterbacks on its All-Time Team. Brady was the only one currently playing on Sundays, joining retired legends Baugh, Graham, Unitas, Staubach, Montana, Elway, Marino, Favre, and Manning. "Very surreal for me to be part of that. It's an incredible honor," said Brady, a unanimous choice. "I would never have imagined that in my life."

One can talk all day about the "debates" that surround Brady. It is difficult to discuss his individual success without pointing toward the system employed by Belichick. Quarterback is the most difficult position in team sports. There are too many factors involving the team element to allow for one player to dominate football, yet Brady does. His toughness is beyond question. Teammates marvel at his pocket coolness in those scrambled moments in which the quarterback has to be the only one standing still in the middle of what is really little more than an organized riot. And opponents respect his ability to take a pounding and come back at them again on the next play.

Chris Canty of the Dallas Cowboys bore witness to just how tough Brady is during a game against the Patriots, on October 14, 2007. "I came free on a zero blitz," Canty recalled. "I hit Tom Brady harder than I've ever hit any human being on or off the field. And I was like, 'Guys, I got him. . . . There's no way he's getting up from that one.' " Canty was sure he'd knocked Brady out of the game with his monster hit. Then he saw Brady, with the help of a teammate, being peeled off the turf, watching in amazement as the quarterback "got up, shook his head, and called up the huddle. . . . From that moment on, Tom Brady had my utmost respect."

For the record, Brady completed 31 of 46 passes for 388 yards and 5 scores in New England's 48–27 rout of Dallas. Canty admired the effort. "I knew I gave him my best shot, and he took it in stride and he bounced back," he said.

CHAPTER 11
BRADY AND BELICHICK

NEW ENGLAND'S VICTORY OVER INDIANAPOLIS IN THE AFC title game following the 2014 season caused quite a hullaballoo, giving birth to Deflategate, one of the most bizarre controversies in the league's one-hundred-year history, and prompting NFL commissioner Roger Goodell to investigate whether or not a minor rule concerning the air pressure of game-used footballs was circumvented.

"Ask any quarterback, and this is a nonissue," said four-time Pro Bowl quarterback Rich Gannon. "Everybody does something to them. It's like a pitcher; he wants the ball a certain way." It was absurd for anyone to seriously suggest that the pressure of the footballs, however they became deflated, really influenced the outcome of the Patriots' 45–7 crushing of the Colts. It was also farcical to think about penalizing Brady, since there was no evidence to prove he broke any NFL rules regarding the condition of the footballs. "For guys to stand up and say that he cheated and that he's lying about it without having all the facts in hand, I think that's pretty irresponsible. I really do," said former Patriots' QB Drew Bledsoe in Brady's defense.

The effects of underinflated footballs dragged on for nearly two years. The matter finally being resolved, Tom Brady accepted a four-game suspension and sat out the start of the 2016 season. While his teammates were winning 3 games and losing 1, Brady was doing everything he could to make his body feel like

The Patriots were forced to play someone other than Tom Brady at quarterback for the first four games of the 2016 season. AP PHOTO / ELISE AMENDOLA

he was playing football. Wearing a helmet and shoulder pads, he went through the usual quarterback drills. Assistant coaches batted him with padded arms and bags as he threw. Brady recruited receivers, including former teammate Wes Welker, to run routes for him and help during the downtime.

"We trained harder than the sport itself demands," said Alex Guerrero, Brady's body coach.

The quarterback's focus was on being a leader, not a martyr.

"He's got a tremendous sense of the present. He doesn't get rattled," said his father, Tom Sr. "He's got a peaceful demeanor. He's pretty clear-thinking and analytical."

Brady returned to the starting lineup in Week 5 having missed the first month of the season. By the second month, he was ready. Ready to throw touchdown passes. In fact, he tossed 12 TD passes in the first 4 games, with no interceptions, and a passer rating of nearly 134. Brady was honored for his personal comeback with a trophy as Player of the Month for October—winning the award a ninth time, more than anyone else. November wasn't too shabby, either. He threw 4 scoring passes to four different receivers—Julian Edelman, Malcolm Mitchell, James White, and Danny Amendola—in a 30–17 Week 11 win against the 49ers in San Francisco.

For Brady it was all about winning, as usual. With their trusted QB back under center, the Pats won 11 of 12 games, and finished the season with an NFL-best 14-2 record. After reclaiming command of the offense, Brady threw for 28 touchdowns (in just 12 games), with only 2 interceptions, and a 112.2 passer rating, second best in the league. Such an outstanding season put TB12 in the MVP conversation; he finished as runner-up. The winner was Atlanta QB Matt Ryan, whose MVP selection set the stage for a perfect drama, since the Falcons, as NFC champions, would be facing off against the Patriots in Super Bowl LI at NRG Stadium in Houston, Texas.

Brady never chokes, but he seemed to be caught off guard during the first day of Super Bowl LI media week. He showed rare emotion while answering the question from a seven-year-old boy who won a contest to be a Super Bowl reporter. The boy, who was sitting on the shoulders of former NFL quarterback Trent Dilfer, asked who Brady's hero was. "Who's my hero?" Brady said. "That's a great question. I think my dad is my hero, because he's someone I looked up to every day and . . ." Brady trailed off. He paused, and his eyes welled up. "My dad."

It had been a difficult year for the Patriots' quarterback. Brady's mom, Galynn, was diagnosed with breast cancer in the summer of 2016, and the Super Bowl in Houston was the first game she would be able to attend that season after five months of chemotherapy and radiation treatments. In fact, she finished up treatment just two weeks before the big game. Galynn Brady had been in a grueling fight, and before the game her only son told owner Robert Kraft, "Let's win one for her." The dutiful son would not disappoint.

ONE FOR THE THUMB

The key matchup for Super Bowl LI featured the Falcons' No. 1 scoring offense versus the Patriots' No. 1 scoring defense. Something had to give. The Falcons' offense struck first by exploding for 21 unanswered points in the second quarter. A bullying Atlanta pass rush kept Brady from getting comfortable in the pocket and doing Brady things. He even had helped the underdogs' cause by throwing a ghastly interception that was returned for an Atlanta touchdown. The Falcons scored again on Ryan's second touchdown, at the 8:31 mark of the third quarter, to extend the lead to 28–3. Ryan's MVP award was looking well deserved. But

Brady exhorted his teammates to play harder and tougher, to give more.

Brady never panicked. He exhorted his teammates to play harder and tougher, to give more. The Patriots shored up holes in their offensive line, and Brady began finding openings in the Atlanta secondary and completing passes. Lots of 'em. Soon the deficit was cut to 28–9. And then 28–12. And then 28–20. With fifty-seven seconds left in regulation the score was tied, 28–28. And then 8 plays into overtime it was Patriots 34, Falcons 28. And it was over. That fast.

The first overtime game in Super Bowl history ended with a total of 31 team and individual records either set or matched. James White's 14 receptions and 20 points scored (based on 3 touchdowns and a 2-point conversion) were among the broken records. Brady, for orchestrating the epic comeback, was named the game's MVP for a record fourth time. He threw the ball 62 times

Tom Brady pulled the Patriots out of a 25-point hole and beat the Falcons in Super Bowl LI.
AP PHOTO / DARRON CUMMINGS

and completed 43. He passed for 466 yards, yet his longest completion was only for 28 yards.

This triumph, the quarterback's fifth career championship, was surely one of the sweetest, if not *the* sweetest, of them all. Brady was never going to give up, even though the deck was stacked against him. Facing a 25-point deficit with about twenty-one minutes to play, he reached deep within himself and led the Patriots on a 31–0 run that would turn a Super Bowl–record deficit into a victory. He threw a pair of touchdown passes down the stretch, not to mention the decisive 2-point conversion completion to Danny Amendola inside the final minute of the game. New England made one stunning play after another, beating all odds to achieve what is considered the greatest comeback in NFL history.

"Come on, man, when it was 28–3, I'm thinking what you and everybody else was thinking—that we pretty much had this game," Falcons receiver Mohamed Sanu said. "Tom Brady just took it to the next level. He made some great plays."

But the greatest comeback in Super Bowl history may never have happened, and the Patriots wouldn't have been Super Bowl champions, if wide receiver Julian Edelman hadn't made a mind-boggling, gravity-defying, jaw-dropping catch late in the fourth quarter. It's a play that will be on highlight reels for years to come. Brady dropped back to pass with 2:28 to play, trailing by 8 points, 64 yards from the end zone. The first player to touch the quarterback's pass was a Falcons' defender who tipped the ball but couldn't pull it in. The ball spun around, end over end, through the air. As it tumbled toward the ground, Edelman, outnumbered and surrounded, fought off three Falcons players—even going through the legs of one of them—twice bobbling the ball in midair before landing, and somehow scooping it up before it hit the ground.

"It was one of the greatest catches I've ever seen," said Brady. "I don't know how the hell he caught it." The 23-yard circus catch gave the Patriots a crucial first down from their own 36. Four plays later, New England scored, tying the game at 28 and forcing overtime.

New England has been on the wrong end of spectacular plays—David Tyree, Mario Manningham, Jermaine Kearse—but a Patriot finally made a miraculous Super Bowl catch that benefited New England for a change. "Yeah, I couldn't believe it," said Brady. "We've been on the other end of a few of those catches and tonight, you know, we came up with it. It was a pretty spectacular catch."

The euphoria on the New England sideline lasted several minutes. Then came the annual handoff of the Super Bowl trophy. Brady, thirty-nine, could barely contain his emotions as he soaked under a rain of red, white, and blue confetti. NFL commissioner Roger Goodell invited the Patriots to "come on up and get your trophy." All week long Goodell had speculated that the possibility of such a moment would not be awkward. He was wrong about that. Eventually, Brady could share the moment with the people who are most important in his life: his wife, Gisele, and their kids, Benjamin and Vivian, and his oldest son, Jack. He held his young daughter, who was wearing her dad's replica jersey, and gave his wife a passionate kiss. Then Brady shared an emotional moment with his mom on the field. Galynn wore a bandanna to cover her head and a No. 12 shirt that read BRADY'S LADIES on the back.

The big win was extra special for Brady's mom, and a reminder of how sweet this Super Bowl victory really was.

With a victory in Super Bowl LI, Brady won "one for the thumb," and was now as firmly associated with big-game brilliance as anyone who has ever played the game. And yet, if you asked the five-time Super Bowl winner which ring was his favorite, the underdog-turned-ultimate-winner would give you an answer that displays his ultra-competitive mind-set: "You know what my favorite Super Bowl ring is? The next one."

In the off-season, the forty-year-old Brady became the oldest player to grace the cover of *Madden NFL*, but he did not succumb to its "curse." Instead, he also became the oldest player to lead the league in passing yardage and was named MVP for a third time.

¡VIVA BRADY!

The defending champions weren't showing signs of suffering from a Super Bowl hangover at the start of the 2017 campaign. A trip to New Orleans in Week 2 to visit the Saints turned out to be the perfect tonic for Brady. He threw 3 touchdown passes in the first quarter alone, passed for 300 yards by halftime, and New England scored 30 first-half points before coasting to the finish. Brady ended the game having completed 30 of 39 passes for 447 yards, with 3 scores and no interceptions, establishing an NFL record with his 52nd game with 3 or more TDs and 0 INTs. He was named Player of the Week for his performance in the 36–20 win against the Saints, the 28th time he has received the honor, moving out of a tie with Peyton Manning for the most in NFL history. At age forty, the

Patriots quarterback showed no signs of slowing down in a game dominated by younger players.

Brady at full tilt had been lighting up scoreboards in NFL stadiums around the country for years. Why should this year be any different? He started the 2017 season on a torrid pace, throwing for 24 touchdowns to just 3 interceptions through the first 11 games.

Brady made his first sojourn to Mexico to play at high altitude a successful one by throwing for 339 yards and 3 touchdowns in New England's 33–8 victory over the Oakland Raiders, in Week 11. The New England quarterback completed his first 12 passes, and picked apart Oakland's defense to chants of "Brady! Brady!" from an amped-up crowd at Azteca Stadium, in Mexico City.

Brady felt right at home, south of the border, in what was technically a Raiders home game, but a sore Achilles that began to ache in Mexico hobbled Brady for the rest of the season. The injury limited his mobility but not his ability to throw passes under duress with accuracy. Brady led the NFL in passing yards in 2017, throwing for 4,577 yards alongside 32 touchdowns, 8 interceptions, and a 102.8 passer rating en route to leading New England to its ninth consecutive division title. NFL.com's Gil Brandt said Brady "carried one of the least-talented Patriots team he's played with" to a 13-3 record, marking eight years in a row the Pats reached at least 12 wins in a season.

Tom Brady was named the NFL's Most Valuable Player for the third time in his career, and ten years after he won his first. He joined an exclusive club, with Jim Brown, Brett Favre, and Johnny Unitas, who also won the most prestigious individual NFL award three times. Peyton Manning is the all-time leader, with five MVP awards. Brady, forty, also was the oldest player ever to be named. "Tom has been able to push the boundary," said backup quarterback Brian Hoyer.

Brady's regular-season act was good enough to earn an MVP award, but he seemed to take his game to another level in the postseason. In three elimination games—win-or-go-home—he threw for 1,132 yards, 8 touchdowns, and no interceptions. The run began with Brady throwing 3 touchdown passes, none longer than 5 yards, to thump Tennessee, 35–14, in the divisional round. But then, Brady suffered a bloody injury to his throwing hand when he attempted a handoff to Rex Burkhead in practice. Brady came away from the exchange screaming in pain. The gash near his right thumb required a dozen stitches and compelled Brady to wear red gloves to his press conferences to prevent cameras from getting a clear shot. When the quarterback was asked one too many questions about his hand, he snapped.

"I'm not talking about it," he said.

Brady would do his talking on the field.

The crowd at Gillette Stadium cheered loudly as Tom Brady emerged from the locker room and jogged onto the field for pregame warm-ups. Everyone noticed Brady was wearing black tape over the inside part of his injured right hand—but no glove. By now, Brady's hand had become the most scrutinized body part in Boston since Red Sox pitcher Curt Schilling's right ankle tendon—the bloody sock—in the 2004 playoffs.

"He's No. 1 because of the production [and] the individual statistics. He's had a revolving door in terms of the supporting cast around him from year to year, and yet he doesn't miss a beat."

—KIRK COUSINS, PRO BOWL QB

With Brady in the starting lineup, CBS play-by-play man, Jim Nantz, called the AFC Championship Game between the heavily favored Patriots and the Jacksonville Jaguars, a "David vs. Goliath matchup," and for about fifty-one minutes, David was winning. Goliath trailed by 10 points, with only nine minutes left in the fourth quarter, and with the clock ticking down, the team was up against it. The Patriots needed two scores to stay in the game. Brady shook off the hand injury and threw 2 touchdown passes to Danny Amendola, the go-ahead score coming with 2:48 remaining in the game—and possibly the season.

Brady rallied the Patriots back to the Super Bowl with a 24–20 comeback victory. He finished 26 of 38 for 290 yards and 2 touchdowns, four days after a freak accident at practice produced a major scare. Storybook stuff. Moments after the thrilling finish, CBS Sports.com tweeted out a lasting image of Brady with the tagline "All He Does Is Win." The taming of the Jaguars was a fantastic feat,

Tom Brady and Bill Belichick are both heading to the Pro Football Hall of Fame, and one would not be in position to make it without the other. AP PHOTO / CHARLES KRUPA

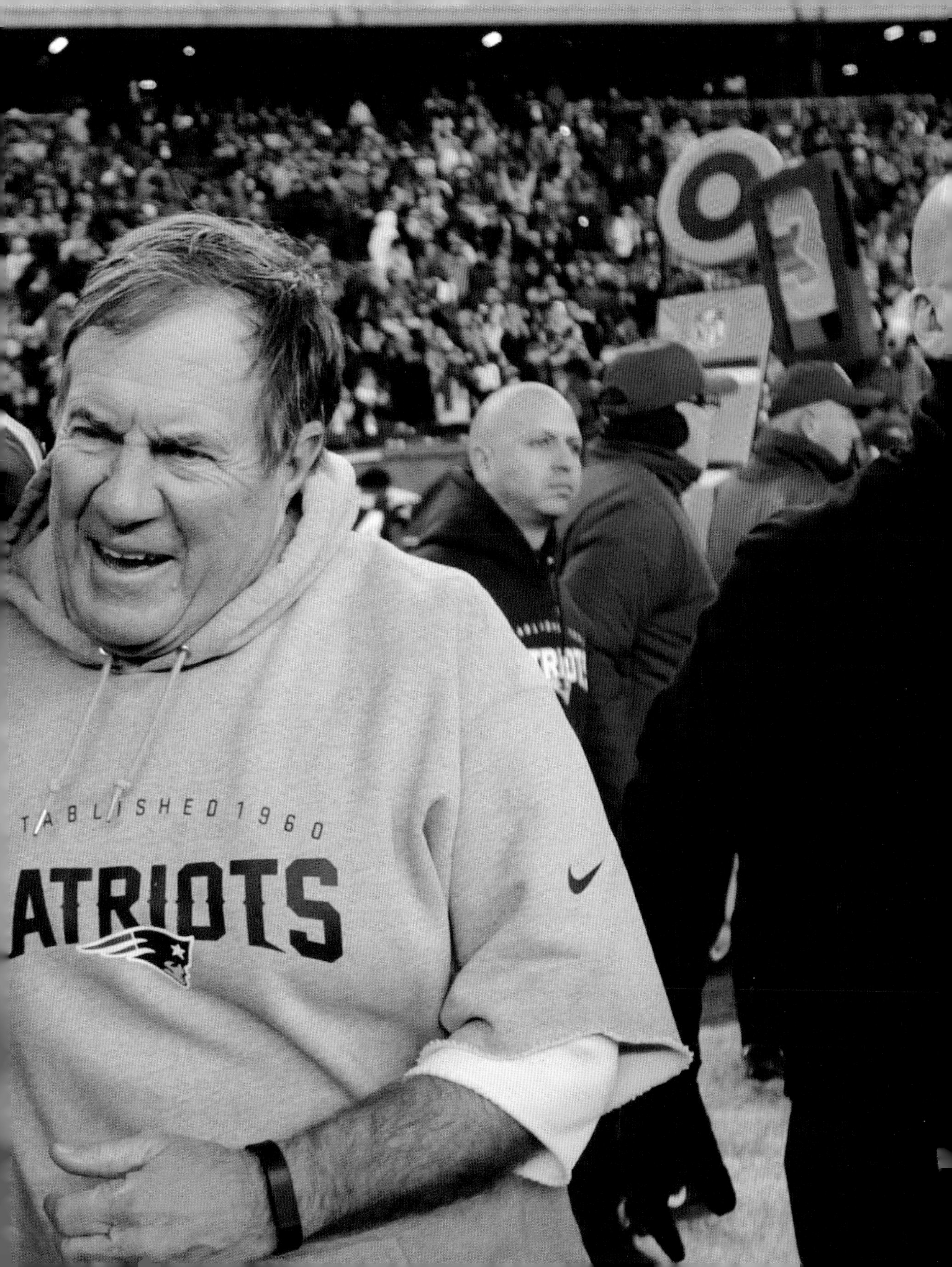
TABLISHED 1960
ATRIOTS

marking the 54th time that Brady had engineered a game-winning performance to lead the Patriots to a victory from a fourth-quarter deficit or tie. Of those 54 winning drives by Brady, 11 had come in the playoffs. Such clutch performances in games with the highest stakes are why many view Brady as the greatest quarterback of all time.

"Tommy's the best. He's the toughest guy I've ever met, physically [and] mentally," said Danny Amendola, who had 7 catches for 84 yards and 2 touchdowns.

Special-teams captain Matthew Slater said the 54 comebacks are reflective of a once-in-a-lifetime player.

"Tom Brady. He's one of a kind," said Slater, one of the Patriots' emotional leaders.

MAN IN THE HOODIE

During the postgame press conference, when asked to describe Brady's gutsy performance with a hand injury, Belichick's demeanor turned tougher than a $2 steak. "Tom did a great job, and he's a tough guy," said the coach. "We all know that, all right? But we're not talking about open heart surgery here." Belichick was sending his quarterback to their eighth Super Bowl together with a psychological kick in the pants. Brady, former seventh-stringer at Michigan, had grown accustomed to the feeling.

Belichick made a habit of chastising his quarterback on Monday mornings in front of the entire team while reviewing game film. New England could win by 3 touchdowns and Belichick would still hunt down the two or three plays Brady had mismanaged, which under different circumstances could've cost the Patriots the game, or their season. Belichick employed a tough-love style with Brady because he knew he could yell at his quarterback and Brady could take it. The greater message is being delivered to the team: If the coach can yell at a sure-fire Hall of Famer, everyone else had best be mindful. For the better part of two decades, none of it bothered Brady, because all he wants to do is win. "He's a no-nonsense coach," Brady said. "He's always got his foot on the gas pedal."

Brady and Belichick are the most successful coach-quarterback combination in NFL history. Including postseason, they've won 249 games together, and that is No. 1 in the NFL since the 1970 merger. Drew Brees and Sean Payton are next, with a distant 151.

They won six Super Bowls together, two more than Chuck Noll and Terry Bradshaw, and three more than Bill Walsh and Joe Montana.

Brady has called Belichick the best coach in league history, and "an incredible mentor to me," recognizing that he never could have built such a legendary career without his hoodie-wearing Yoda. Belichick appreciates Brady's attention to every little detail and returns the compliment. "I love coaching Tom," Belichick said. "Nobody works harder or prepares better."

"He has a management style [with] players," Brady said of Belichick, "and he would say, 'Look, I'm not the easiest coach to play for.' I would agree. He's not the easiest coach to play for."

The relationship between Brady and his curmudgeonly coach, though tested at times, was never truly adversarial.

"We've had a great relationship," Brady said. "A very respectful relationship for a long time."

> "If you've got to say 'Who's the best of all time?'—well, given the numbers, and the championships, Tom is."
> —JOE NAMATH,
> HALL OF FAME QB

Together, with Robert Kraft, they built and maintained an eighteen-year dynasty—winning 17 division titles and averaging 12.2 regular-season wins a year over that period—at a time when the NFL uses the salary cap, the draft, the schedule, and free agency as weapons to prevent franchises from doing just that. In fact, no team has won back-to-back NFL titles since the Pats did it following the 2003 and '04 seasons.

The two pillars of New England's dynasty are inextricably linked. It's a lock that Brady and Belichick are both heading to the Pro Football Hall of Fame, and there's a good chance one would not have been in position to make it without the other. "Put it this way," Belichick told author Gary Myers. "Without Tom Brady, I wouldn't have accomplished a fraction of what I've accomplished. There is simply no other quarterback I'd rather have than Tom Brady. I can't say any more about a player than that."

Brady's predecessor, Drew Bledsoe, has a surprising perspective on the Patriots' formula for success since his playing days in New England. In assessing Belichick's achievements, Bledsoe told ESPN in 2020, "It would be really hard for him to do what he does without those two [Brady and Kraft] bracketing him. Kraft supplies the heart and soul. He really loves his players. And then he's got Tommy, who still has an underdog's chip on his shoulder twenty years in."

STILL STYLIN'

Tom Brady was continuing to test the conventional wisdom about the maximum age at which an NFL quarterback can remain effective. He rallied the Patriots to two fourth-quarter touchdowns in less than six minutes against Jacksonville, and punched New England's ticket back to the Super Bowl. Brady's Patriots were going to have an opportunity to win three championships in four seasons, thirteen years after they did it the first time around. The game against the Philadelphia Eagles would be played at a neutral site, US Bank Stadium in Minneapolis, but for Brady, it would feel more like a home game, relatively speaking. That's because Brady, even though he grew up in California, has said he's "half Minnesotan. That really is my roots, and it's very much a part of who I am." His mother, Galynn, grew up in Browerville, a small town 135 miles away. It's a place he visited every summer, and sometimes in the winter, since he was a baby. It's also where Brady's parents got married in 1969.

This trip to Minnesota, however, was all business. Brady didn't have a chance to get to Browerville as he prepared for the Super Bowl. As for tickets, they were pretty tough to come by, Brady said, "but I'm trying the best I can to accommodate everybody."

Super Bowl LII will be remembered as one of the best ever. Statistically, it *was* the best ever. New England and Philadelphia combined to produce the most total yards in a game in NFL history, racking up an eye-popping 1,151 yards in the

This jersey—worn by Tom Brady while setting the career record for wins by a quarterback—quickly made it to the Pro Football Hall of Fame, in Canton, Ohio. AP PHOTO / ELISE AMENDOLA

contest. That total included 505 yards passing from Brady, who shredded his own previous record of 466 set the previous year in Super Bowl LI. Although Brady lived up to his big-game reputation, Brady & Co. weren't able to tame the Eagles. The Patriots lost, 41–33. It was no consolation that New England's 33 points were the most scored in a loss in Super Bowl history.

"This is not the Harlem Globetrotters versus the Washington Generals," said Brady, who in the process became the first quarterback to break 10,000 postseason passing yards. "This is all about tough competition against the best teams. They deserved it."

Philadelphia's quarterback, Nick Foles, won the game's Most Valuable Player award after he threw for 373 yards and 3 touchdowns with 1 interception, and also caught a 9-yard touchdown pass on a trick play that became known as the Philly Special.

A few months after the Super Bowl, *Sports Illustrated* released its Fashionable 50 issue, identifying the trendsetters and statement-makers of the sports world. Though Odell Beckham Jr. walked away with the title of Most Fashionable Athlete, it was no surprise to those in the know, in terms of fashion, that Brady landed in the Timeless Style category. He was in good company, alongside Henrik Lundqvist, Roger Federer, and P. K. Subban.

Did the style award lessen the sting of a Super Bowl loss? Certainly not. But it helped demonstrate that Brady still had pop-culture relevance. As the 2018 season approached, he set his sights on proving his relevance on the football field as well.

STAYING POWER

Tom Brady turned forty-one on August 3, one month before New England played its 2018 season-opener. He was eight years older than his two next-oldest teammates. On the day the youngest Patriot, linebacker Ja'Whaun Bentley, was born, Brady was nineteen, and about to start the season as a backup quarterback at the University of Michigan. Thirty of his teammates were closer in age to Brady's eleven-year-old son Jack than they were to Brady himself. "We joke about it. He's forty-one, but he's really twenty-four," Brian Hoyer said.

Brady, playing in his seventeenth season, joined a very exclusive club during the second half of New England's 38–24 Week 5 victory over the Colts. Brady became only the third quarterback in NFL history to record 500 career touchdown passes when he tossed a 34-yard bomb to wide receiver Josh Gordon in the end zone during the fourth quarter. Gordon was the seventy-first different receiver to catch a TD pass from Brady, breaking Testaverde's previous NFL record, of 70.

Of all the Brady records, this is perhaps the most unique, as it speaks to Brady's longevity—the fact that he was able to set the mark while playing for just one team. By contrast, the previous recordholder, Vinny Testaverde, played for seven different clubs during his NFL career, from 1987 to 2007.

The following week, the Patriots' quarterback led his team to a dramatic 43–40 victory over Patrick Mahomes and the Chiefs at Gillette Stadium, becoming one of four players with 200 career regular-season wins, and the first quarterback. By adding the 27 wins for his accomplishments in the postseason, Brady moved past Adam Vinatieri for the most career wins ever by an NFL player.

Brady's stat line took a slight dip in 2018. He threw for 4,355 yards with 29 touchdowns and 11 interceptions. He made some uncharacteristic plays throughout the season, threw some awful interceptions, and missed some wide-open receivers. This is a level of play that New England fans definitely weren't used to. But Brady is able to get things done when it matters most. Even though the regular season wasn't an easy one, he managed to lead the Patriots to an 11-5 record and their NFL-record tenth-consecutive AFC East title. Brady's ability to perform in clutch situations hadn't changed, though. The Patriots defeated the Los Angeles Chargers handily, 41–28, in the divisional round, setting up a much-anticipated rematch against the Chiefs in the AFC Championship Game, in Kansas City.

The Chiefs were led by their MVP QB, Mahomes, in just his second year in the NFL, and his first as a starter. Mahomes had a breakout season, throwing for

5,097 yards and a league-leading 50 touchdowns. The dominant storyline was how this game represented a passing of the torch, from Brady to Mahomes, and the Patriots to the Chiefs. But that must have lit a fire under the Pats. The team that has been there, done that—and done it again and again—survived a scare that felt like a cold slap in the face.

The temperature dropped to 18 degrees with a wind-chill factor of 8 midway through the fourth quarter of the title game at Arrowhead Stadium, before 77,034 red-clad, frozen fans. But the Pats were just getting warmed up. A pair of high-powered offenses led by superstar quarterbacks at the opposite ends of their careers combined for 31 points and 4 lead changes in the final seven minutes of regulation, sending the AFC title game into overtime. From there, Brady, the forty-one-year-old New England quarterback, who turned the last-minute, game-winning drive into an art form, took over. The Patriots won the overtime coin toss and Brady marched the team downfield, converting 3 huge third-and-10 plays on a 75-yard drive that ended with Rex Burkhead's 2-yard touchdown run and a 37–31 victory.

> The Patriots have been there, done that—and done it again and again.

Brady's heroics—it was the twelfth winning drive in the postseason in the fourth quarter or overtime—sent New England to its NFL-record eleventh Super Bowl in franchise history. Brady and Belichick hugged for photographers in the postgame celebration, and NFL Network microphones picked up an emotional on-field exchange between them in which the coach told his quarterback, "I love ya, man," and Brady made a similar remark back. The greatest QB-coach combination in the modern football era was heading to its ninth Super Bowl overall, their fifth of the decade, their fourth in the past five years, and their third in a row. Not only was nine Super Bowl appearances more than any other coach-quarterback duo in history, it was more Super Bowl appearances than any other *franchise*. "Overtime, on the road against a great team," said Brady, who was 30 of 46 for 348 yards against the Chiefs. "They had no quit. Neither did we. We played our best football at the end."

The next day, he posted a video to Instagram of himself and Gronkowski walking to the team bus after the game. Both are smiling, and Gronk flashes his AFC championship T-shirt. It was a humble brag that Brady has steered away from in the past. But he acknowledged after the AFC title win that he was "as excited as I have been in a long time. When you have 70,000 people cheering against you, it is pretty sweet when you win on the road," Brady said. On Twitter, congratulations came from all corners of New England. Among them was one from Paul Pierce, who helped lead the Celtics to the NBA championship in 2008. "There's aliens, there's Pegasus, and there's Tom Brady," Pierce wrote.

> "He's an alien! I don't even think he's from this universe."
> —KENNY BRITT, EX-NFL WR

CRUNCH TIME

Somehow, the Patriots got it into their heads that no one believed they could win against the Los Angeles Rams in Super Bowl LIII. That mentality clearly motivated Brady. "The odds were stacked against us," he said. "It hasn't been that way for us in a while, and it certainly was this year."

But with New England making its third straight trip to the Super Bowl and its ninth overall in the Brady-Belichick era, it was a tough argument to buy. There's also the fact that the Patriots beat the Chiefs, 37–31, on the road in overtime. What kind of underdog makes a statement win like that? But Brady and his teammates clung to their underdog status, billing the game against the Rams as the Old Guys versus the Young. The age difference between Tom Brady (forty-one) and the Rams' starting quarterback, Jared Goff (twenty-four), was more than seventeen years. That was the largest gap between starting quarterbacks in Super Bowl history. And they weren't the only big-name, old–young opposing pair at the same position. At thirty-two, the Rams' Sean McVay was the youngest head coach in the NFL, and the youngest to ever lead a team to the Super Bowl. At sixty-six, Bill Belichick was the NFL's longest-tenured coach. And with age and experience come wisdom and a handful of Super Bowl titles.

The New England Patriots won a sixth Super Bowl title in the Tom Brady–Bill Belichick era. The Patriots beat the Rams, 13–3, scoring the go-ahead touchdown with seven minutes left after a grinder of a game in which neither team could sustain offensive drives. Though the Patriots' dynasty was already the greatest in NFL history, winning yet another title only put the team's legacy even further ahead of the pack. New England's defense stepped up in a major way at Mercedes-Benz Stadium in Atlanta, Georgia, holding the Rams to 14 first downs and 260 yards, in the lowest-scoring Super Bowl ever. The fun stat of the game is that it featured the fewest points ever scored by the Patriots in the Brady-Belichick era, yet stands as the largest margin of victory the team's ever had in the Super Bowl.

Brady was 21 for 35 for 262 yards and 1 interception. He didn't throw a touchdown, but he didn't need to. He engineered a pair of fourth-quarter scoring drives that helped the Patriots pull away for the win, giving the quarterback an incredible sixth Super Bowl victory—the most for any player, at any position. Vintage Brady showed up at Super Bowl LIII briefly. With under ten minutes remaining in the fourth quarter, Brady went 4-for-4 passing on the winning drive. It's what you expect from Brady. A sweet touch pass over a defender to Rob Gronkowski for 18 yards. Then a 13-yarder to Super Bowl MVP Julian Edelman. A dump-off 7-yard play to Rex Burkhead. Then Brady completed the most crucial pass of the game, a 29-yard toss to Gronkowski, to set up a short dive for the winning touchdown.

It wasn't the most spectacular drive of his career, but it was Brady being Brady. Masterful reads. Pinpoint accuracy. Clutch throws. And perhaps therein lies the crux of Brady's greatness. For as many memorable games and thrilling comebacks as he has produced, Brady doesn't really have a signature play. His most memorable moments—all of those Super Bowl–winning drives—were, instead, collections of fairly unremarkable moments that culminated in greatness. Those drives aren't special because of some ridiculous degree of difficulty Brady overcame. They're special for the opposite reason; they're special because of how easy he made it look as he coldly dissected championship-level defenses in crunch time.

Tom Brady and his daughter, Vivian, amid the confetti celebration after the Patriots' Super Bowl LIII win.
DAMIAN STROHMEYER VIA AP

Fourth-quarter comebacks, game-winning drives, and Super Bowl victories are what define a quarterback as clutch in the NFL. Brady could now boast of authoring game-winning drives in the fourth quarter or overtime of six different Super Bowls. Nobody else has had more than six game-winning drives in the *postseason* since 1970. Brady has 14 such drives in the postseason.

Tom Brady has stood the test of time. When he won his first Super Bowl, he was the youngest quarterback to hold the trophy. When he won his sixth, he was the oldest quarterback to win it all. By age thirty-three, Brady already was a three-time Super Bowl champion and winner of two MVP awards. Since the season he played at age thirty-seven, he has won an MVP award, claimed three more Super Bowl titles, and played in another, putting up the best single statistical game of his career.

"It's an absolute honor to play with a guy like Tom," said Edelman. "Anyone that gets to play with that man understands why he is the way he is."

CHAPTER 12
CANTON CALLING

THE NEW ENGLAND PATRIOTS UNVEILED THE TEAM'S SIXTH Super Bowl championship banner prior to the 2019 season home-opener at Gillette Stadium, and then the forty-two-year-old quarterback Tom Brady did what Brady always does in a 33–3 beatdown of the Pittsburgh Steelers. He threw for 3 touchdowns and 341 interception-free yards. He threw the long ball with the eagerness of a man half his age. He beat a defense that included Pittsburgh's first-round pick, linebacker Devin Bush, a lifetime after beating a Cleveland defense that included Bush's father during New England's first title season in 2001.

Brady made his seventeenth Opening Day start, and outside of his lost 2008 season and his four-game suspension in 2016, he hasn't missed any time. Worse yet, for long-suffering fans of division opponents, Brady has publicly entertained the idea of playing beyond his forty-fifth birthday. And he probably can. He's in the best physical shape of his life: He's perfected his diet, his arm is more accurate, and his decision-making is smarter. He's ageless, and spends his entire waking life training with one goal in mind: to keep playing football. And to play winning football.

Almost everyone has an explanation for Brady's indomitable success—his coach, the defense, new rules to protect the quarterback, luck, the soft schedule of a perennially underachieving division—but one of the more-valid ones is Brady's devotion to personal sacrifice and unselfishness, traits used to describe the impressive levels of winning, accountability, and team-first culture

Tom Brady lives his life with one goal in mind: to play football and win games. DAVID DUROCHIK VIA AP

embodied by Brady's example since the quarterback came into the league in 2000.

"More times than not," said safety Duron Harmon, "everybody just falls in. It's hard to be an outcast here because it starts at the top. Everybody's doing everything the right way. Tom, he's an unselfish player, and it just trickles down. It's hard to not fit in here." Dan Connolly, the man who snapped the ball to Brady from 2009 to '14, can sum it up better: "It's doing what's best for the team. It's not doing what's best for you; [it's] putting the team first and doing your job."

Brady is undoubtedly the greatest quarterback to ever strap on a helmet. His ability to produce and win games over the past two decades continues to amaze.

"He's an inspiration," said teammate Ben Watson. "I'm going to be telling my grandkids about [him]." Start with the Super Bowls. Brady is Lord of the (Super Bowl) Rings. He's appeared in ten, and won seven, taking home the trophy as the best player in the game five times. Name a Super Bowl record, he owns it. There is still time for Brady to add to his Super Bowl accomplishments and build onto his otherworldly legacy as an immortal player.

But Brady's success doesn't just start and end with the Super Bowl. He's appeared in 45 postseason games—playing in more postseason games than 27 current franchises—and his team has come out on top in 34 of those games, a remarkable .756 winning percentage. He's been to the playoffs so many times, and dominated those games so many times, that he owns a number of postseason records as well, including wins, touchdowns, passing yards, and most starts in a league championship game. These records are reflective of both individual and team success; to make the playoffs and keep coming back every single year, you have to be doing something right.

Brady is no slouch in the regular season, either. In 301 games, he has thrown for 79,204 yards, 581 touchdowns, and only 191 interceptions. His longevity and incredible output during his two decades as an NFL starting quarterback has put him near the top of nearly every conceivable all-time ranking among players at his position, including passing yards, touchdowns, and passer rating. He's won more NFL games than any player in history. He's a three-time All-Pro, with fourteen Pro Bowl selections, though he never attends, once berating teammate Brandon Spikes, "You think I play this *$#& to go to Pro Bowls?"

More often than not, Brady doesn't play in Pro Bowls because he and his team are preparing for the Super Bowl, played the following week. It only seems like Brady's teams are playing on Super Sunday every year. His teams have never had a losing season with Brady as starter (since 2001), winning sixteen division titles, the most by any signal caller. Thanks to his on-field leadership and personal magnetism, winning football games has been a natural law in Foxborough and Tampa. Brady explained his leadership style to Terry Bradshaw of Fox Sports in an interview that aired before Super Bowl LI.

"You get in the huddle and you call those plays, you have ten other guys feelin' your energy. And what are you putting off? Are you putting off confidence? Are you putting off fear? You know they can feel that. And when they get in the huddle with me, I want to look in their eyes, and I want them to feel a belief that we're gonna do it."

Consider the quarterback's words, broadcast during the pregame leading up to Super Bowl LI, in the context of understanding the fact that New England then won the game in the most dramatic come-from-behind victory in Super Bowl history, 34–28—in the process, earning Brady his fifth Super Bowl championship ring and his fourth Super Bowl MVP award—and Brady's comments take on even greater significance.

Brady's continued ability to lead and inspire teammates more than a decade his junior is a unique skill. "He communicates well with every player," coach Josh McDaniels said. "He's one of the first guys in the building to know a new person's name." Brady's introduction to new players is always the same. At some point after they arrive, Brady seeks them out, walks up, and says plainly, "Hi, I'm Tom Brady."

"The guy is a great quarterback. There is a category that people like to say: 'The Greatest to Ever Play.' He is definitely in that category."

—JOE MONTANA, HALL OF FAME QB

"I'm like, 'I know who you are,'" one such brand-new Patriots player, Phillip Dorsett, recalled with a laugh. "You don't have to introduce yourself."

"Tom adopted a leadership style by which he still has time for everyone," said coach Bill Belichick. "He doesn't put himself above anybody, above the equipment manager, above the guy on the practice squad, or above a defensive player. He has respect for them doing their jobs. He gets on people, not in an overly critical way, but still firm. I don't think he's ever shown up anyone, even though some guys might deserve it."

Nobody understands the team concept better than No. 12. "We're in such an intimate environment with each other," Brady said. "You're at work from six in the morning until four in the afternoon. You're in close proximity to these guys for seven months of the year. It's blood, sweat, and tears in everything you're doing. There is a natural camaraderie and bond that probably few professions get to experience. When you're getting the crap knocked out of you and you look to the guy next to you, you've got to believe that the guy has got your back. That is what makes football really special."

THE G.O.A.T.

How do the all-time greats become the all-time greats? By committing every fiber of their lives to their craft. And that's exactly what Tom Brady has done.

No one has had a better view of Brady's work habits than his former coach, Bill Belichick. "He's not a great natural athlete," Belichick told CNBC in 2017. "He's a very smart, instinctive football player. It's not all about talent. It's about dependability, consistency, and being able to improve. If you work hard, and you're coachable, and you understand what you need to do, you can improve."

Drew Bledsoe echoed those sentiments in 2020. "It's the example he sets for everyone in the building. He's always been kind of a mid- to low-tier talent, but he's at the pinnacle of leadership, and example, and work ethic."

Brady has progressed to the point of no return. He's operating in a stratosphere all to himself. There is talk, legitimate talk, of Brady's ascendancy to G.O.A.T. status: the Greatest of All Time. He certainly has the résumé, which is starting to sound like a broken record: seven Super Bowls, five Super Bowl MVPs, three league MVP awards, fourteen Pro Bowls—did we mention a Comeback Player of the Year award?—more NFL records than you can count, and—we almost forgot—a 1997 College Football National Championship ring.

"Tom Brady's the G.O.A.T.," said Von Miller, a three-time All-Pro linebacker with the Denver Broncos.

But Brady cringes when he's called the greatest of all time, and brushes off talk that he has surpassed his boyhood hero, former 49ers legend Joe Montana, as the greatest quarterback and football player in the game's history.

"I wish you would say, 'You're trash, you're too old, you can't get it done no more,' and I would say, 'Thank you very much. I'm going to prove you wrong.' "

Proving people wrong is Brady's MO. He's been doing it ever since he was forced to fight for snaps at Michigan. And he'll keep doing it, for as long as his body will allow. Already in uncharted territory, Brady has insisted for years that he would like to play until he's at least forty-five years old. That would make him an outlier among quarterbacks. In fact, he will likely pass Steve DeBerg as the oldest quarterback to start a regular-season game. DeBerg was 44 years and 279 days old when he returned from five years of retirement to join the Atlanta Falcons and earned his place in the history books. But DeBerg never played at an

Tom Brady waves good-bye to a Cincinnati crowd on December 15, 2019. The quarterback threw a pair of touchdown passes in the game to move within one of the NFL career record. AP PHOTO / FRANK VICTORES

MVP level, even during his prime. If Brady does indeed play into his mid-forties, and keeps winning at a similar rate, his wins record should appear on one of those "Most Unbreakable Sports Records" lists.

When it comes to appreciating Brady's game, one can point to three key areas: clutch performances on the biggest stage, an innate sense of timing in the passing game, and patience to make the right throw. Durability is another area of note. Brady has started all 16 games in a season 17 times. He'll likely do it next year, and the next. At age forty-three, Brady still was playing football. And playing it very well. Especially for other teams in the AFC, this had to be getting very old. When Brady won his first Super Bowl, we were a year into the George W. Bush administration. There are plenty of defensive backs who were in grade school when Brady stepped into the NFL limelight. And yet here he was, in 2019, in his 20th NFL season, still going strong. A 27–13 Week 8 win over the Browns was the 300th victory of Bill Belichick's head-coaching career over the regular season and postseason, with the first coming as the Browns coach against the Patriots in 1991. In addition to making that history, the win also pushed the Pats' record to 8-0, for the third time in team history. The win guaranteed that the Patriots would finish with a record of at least .500 for the 19th straight season. Each of the other thirty-one NFL teams has had at least one losing season since 2001, the year Brady took over as the Patriots' starting QB.

In 2019, the Patriots followed an 8-0 start by losing three of the next five games on the schedule, with all of those losses coming to AFC division leaders. Nobody expected the Pats to go undefeated, but New England was playing uninspired football. The team's offense looked stuck in the mud, and many fans who two months before had their early-February trips booked to Miami, the host city for Super Bowl LIV, suddenly got a bit edgy. You could hear the whispers about Brady. Too old. Too slow. Washed up. Not the same guy. No longer a top-five quarterback. All of these things were shouted about Brady . . . six years ago.

You might not remember, but the 2013 season spelled the end of Brady and the Patriots dynasty. The team was struggling, Brady was struggling; age had come for the quarterback, like it had for everyone else in the history of sports. You also might remember what happened after that season: Rob Gronkowski got healthy, new weapons were brought in on both sides of the ball, and Brady rededicated himself to improving his mobility and reshaping his body. Then the Patriots kicked off an unprecedented run of success, winning three Super Bowls and making it to another, in the five years that followed. Brady, no longer too old or washed up, had been driving the train.

At a time when the 2019 Patriots' record stood at 10-1, the team lost to the Houston Texans, led by the dazzling QB Deshaun Watson, who grew up idolizing Brady. They followed that up with a second loss in a row, 23–16, to the Kansas City Chiefs, a game in which Brady was wholly outplayed by Patrick Mahomes. As to Brady, fans with short memories said he was too old, too slow, washed up, not the same guy, no longer a top-five quarterback. It's a vicious circle for an athlete navigating a long-lasting career.

And then it was on to Cincinnati for the 10-3 Pats. Brady threw a pair of touchdown passes in a 34–13 victory over the Bengals to move within one of the NFL career record. He had touchdown passes of 23 and 7 yards that left him with 538 for his career, one shy of Peyton Manning's record. The second TD was to N'Keal Harry, No. 75 on the list of different receivers to catch a Brady score. By late fourth quarter, the tens of thousands of cheering Patriots fans that filled the stadium rewarded their beloved quarterback by chanting "Brady! Brady! Brady!" as the minutes ran down.

"That was pretty sweet," Brady said, in gratitude for the legions of stalwarts who had made the trip to Ohio.

With this victory, the Patriots had made the playoffs for eleven consecutive seasons, extending their NFL record. Since 2003, they had won all but one AFC East title. "That's what you play for—you play to keep playing," said Belichick.

Tom Brady once famously said, "When I suck, I'll retire." He certainly doesn't suck, as many QBs would happily take his stat line from the 2019 season: 373-of-613 for 4,057 yards with 24 touchdowns and 8 interceptions. But when the campaign came to an abrupt end, during a rare home playoff loss to the Tennessee Titans, Brady, at forty-two, found himself in an unfamiliar place: without a contract to play next season. It might be unimaginable to consider Brady playing for another NFL team. But in different circumstances, Joe Montana, Peyton Manning, and Brett Favre finished somewhere else. Montana in KC, Manning in Denver, and Favre—who, don't forget, started in Atlanta—ended in New York and Minnesota. All three ended up in Canton, Ohio, wearing a golden jacket and accepting a bust of their likeness, upon induction to the Pro Football Hall of Fame. Soon enough, Tom Brady will be joining them.

Brady is a certain first-ballot, unanimous Hall of Fame selection. Whatever can be achieved as a football player, Brady has pretty much done it. He has provided the sport with some of its most transfixing and spectacular comebacks in the biggest games and on the brightest stages. Perhaps most surprising of all is that at an age when he could easily rest on his laurels, Brady continues to care immensely about his craft. "The true competitors," he says, "are the ones who always play to win."

EPILOGUE

WITH UNDER TEN SECONDS LEFT IN WHAT TURNED OUT TO BE the final game of the New England Patriots' 2019 season, Tom Brady was still trying to figure out what went wrong. A moment earlier, in his final act on the Gillette Stadium field, Brady threw a pass from his end zone that was deflected, then intercepted and returned for a touchdown.

When the final seconds ticked away of the Patriots' 20–13 playoff defeat to the Tennessee Titans, the defending champion Patriots would be denied their quest for a record seventh Super Bowl championship, unceremoniously bounced from the NFL playoffs in the opening round by the lowest-seeded team in their conference. The defeat triggered a stunning and sudden end to a Patriots' season that had begun with such promise, at 8-0.

After the painful loss, Brady sat alone and motionless on the bench, a wounded soldier, his helmet on the ground between his feet. No one spoke to or approached him. He remained altogether still, his eyes staring blindly into space. He had a quizzical expression on his face, which was entirely un-Brady-like. Typically self-assured, Brady looked as if he didn't know exactly what to do, or where to go.

He finally lifted his gaze and began to process the scene around him. When the quarterback at last rose from the bench, he was still alone, and he walked, unaccompanied, off the field, and toward the tunnel, which would take him into the locker room for the final time that season. There would be no embrace with coach Bill Belichick, and no trophy-hoisting under a stream of colored confetti.

The 2019 playoff defeat, some said, signaled the beginning of the end for the celebrated Brady-Belichick partnership, a combination that has made New England America's foremost sports dynasty of this century. But after the game,

Brady was not in the mood for contemplating the moment, or its weight. The quarterback would become a free agent for the first time in his career unless he was signed to a new contract by New England. Since Brady had been unusually vague about his future during the season—and had put his Boston-area mansion up for sale in the summer—there had been much speculation that he might retire. Less than a minute into a news conference following the abrupt playoff exit, Brady was asked if he was going to quit football.

Brady, forty-two, paused, with a faint look of exasperation.

"I would say it's pretty unlikely," he finally said.

Twice he was asked if he wanted to return to the Patriots, or expected to, and his responses seemed to indicate that he didn't know exactly what to say, or perhaps had not made up his mind. Brady praised the owner, the coaches, and his teammates, and said: "I was proud to be a part of this team. Again, I just don't know what's going to happen, and I'm not going to predict it." He added: "I've loved playing for this team for two decades and winning a lot of games. I've always tried to do the right thing. Who knows what the future holds, so we'll leave it at that."

The answer arrived ten weeks later, when Brady shocked the football world by announcing he'd no longer be playing for the Patriots, telling us "my football journey will take place elsewhere." The quarterback delivered the news in a goodbye message posted to his social media accounts. "It is time for me to open a new stage for my life and career." The franchise legend officially parted ways with the only NFL team he'd ever known. The most decorated football player of all time, a New England sports hero on a par with Larry Bird, Bobby Orr, and Carl Yastrzemski, had played his final game with the Patriots. By every measure, March 17, 2020, will be remembered as the saddest St. Patrick's Day in Boston's history.

Three days after announcing his departure from the Patriots, Brady signed a two-year contract worth $50 million to play for the Tampa Bay Buccaneers, an NFC team that hadn't been to the playoffs since the 2007 season. He switched conferences to join a promising roster that looked primed to compete, with a coach, Bruce Arians, who'd been dubbed "the quarterback whisperer"; a strong offensive line; elite receivers; and a young playmaking defense. As an added enticement, Super Bowl LV would be held at Raymond James Stadium, in Tampa, Florida, his new home field. The following month, Rob Gronkowski, a favorite target who has caught more of Brady's career touchdown passes than any other receiver, came out of retirement to join Brady in his new city.

Now the greatest quarterback ever would author the epilogue to his Hall of Fame career as a member of the Buccaneers. But, as has often been the case throughout Brady's career, there were doubters. Before Brady signed with Tampa, Hall-of-Famer Kurt Warner told *USA Today*, "I just think there's a lot to lose here if you're Tom Brady going somewhere else." Brady's boyhood idol, Joe Montana, echoed those sentiments in an interview with NFL Media: "It's not easy to go to another team and get accepted, no matter how much success you've had and how many years you've played." And on March 20, CBS sportswriter Tom Fornelli wrote a Brady piece headlined, "Why Tampa Bay isn't likely to get its money's worth from Future Hall of Famer."

So, entering the season, Brady still had something to prove—including that he could win without Belichick, who had been his only coach in twenty NFL seasons. It didn't take long to prove the doubters wrong. Newly energized in Florida, where Ponce de León once sought the Fountain of Youth, Brady enjoyed a throwback season in 2020. He finished second in the league in touchdown passes (40) and third in passing yards (4,633). With Brady at the helm, the Buccaneers went 11-5, including four straight wins to close out the regular season, and entered the NFL playoffs as the fifth seed in the NFC. New England, meanwhile, fell apart without him. Belichick's Pats were 7-9 and missed the playoffs for the first time in twelve years.

Brady's time with the Patriots will forever be a part of him. Without a doubt, New England's favorite son left one of the biggest impacts we've ever seen on one sports franchise. A fixture of the NFL playoffs this century while winning

Tom Brady and tight end Rob Gronkowski reunited for a championship season in Tampa Bay. PHOTO BY CLIFF WELCH / ICON SPORTSWIRE VIA AP IMAGES

thirty postseason games in a Patriots uniform, he now appeared on television screens each Sunday in the pewter and red colors of the Buccaneers. It was at first a strange feeling to see Brady in a different uniform, but fans may have to adjust to that scene for a while, because Brady has for years indicated that he plans to play until he is forty-five. And who is going to stop him?

"I'm definitely older," Brady said after helping Tampa win its first playoff game in eighteen years, a 31-23 wild card–round victory in Washington, DC. "But I'm hanging in there."

Following the Buccaneers' 30-20 divisional round playoff victory over the Saints in New Orleans, Brady headed to his NFL record fourteenth conference championship game—more than twenty-eight other NFL franchises—and ninth in ten seasons. With the Buccaneers' 31-26 win over the Green Bay Packers (and eventual 2020 MVP Aaron Rodgers) in the NFC championship game, Brady secured his record tenth Super Bowl appearance, and his first with his new team. After the game, Brady found his oldest son, Jack, in the Lambeau Field stands, and told him, "Love you, kiddo! How 'bout that?! We're gonna go to the Super Bowl baby!"

For Brady, this would be his tenth Super Bowl, and his first wearing a skull and crossed sabers on his helmet. On February 7, 2021, at Raymond James Stadium before a socially distanced 24,835 partisan fans, Brady was typical Brady. He was flawless in important situations, efficient in the moments between, as he guided the Buccaneers to a lopsided 31-9 win over the defending champion Kansas City Chiefs and their superstar quarterback Patrick Mahomes. The Bucs played mistake-free football and Brady completed 21 of 29 passes for 201 yards and three touchdowns, including two scoring passes to Gronk, for old times' sake.

The Buccaneers completed a championship run that may never be matched: three playoff wins on the road and a Super Bowl win at home. Brady ousted three Super Bowl-winning quarterbacks along the way, and a singular season ended with the type of celebration—confetti, Gatorade baths, the Lombardi trophy in his hands—that felt so familiar.

After the game, when Arians was asked what Brady had brought with him to Tampa Bay, the coach said: "The belief he gave everybody in the organization that this could be done. It only took one man."

Brady, in a postgame interview, tried to deflect credit for the victory, but there was no question his determination and excellence inspired his new teammates to reach great heights.

"Everybody believed we could win," Brady said after the game. "All year we believed in ourselves."

They believed, surely, largely because they had Brady, and Brady makes people believe. He is someone whose appetite for competition and desire to succeed has not receded over time. That Brady, at forty-three, showed no signs of physical decline was remarkable. That he managed to raise another championship banner barely a year since leaving New England, with a Tampa Bay Buccaneers team that hadn't so much as sniffed the postseason since 2007, was all the more stunning. An ageless Brady proved he could win anywhere.

"I think we knew this was going to happen tonight, didn't we?" Brady said afterward, standing atop a stage as the home crowd cheered.

Maybe he did.

History will consider Super Bowl LV another legacy game for Brady, in that he went from winning his first ring as a Patriot in the season of 9/11 to winning his seventh ring as a Buc during a year upended by the coronavirus pandemic. Through it all, Brady kept collecting rings, and though he won't call this one, accomplished without the genius of Belichick or the influence of the noted "Patriot Way," the sweetest of his seven championships, he won't deny its significance.

"I'm not making any comparisons," Brady said, acting as if his Super Bowls are like children. "This team is world champion forever. You can't take it away from us."

For now, much to his opponents' dismay, Brady is not going away. With his first title outside New England, Brady brought to a boil the long-simmering debate about sports' greatest athlete. That discussion must include Brady. The ultimate winner, Brady is an NFL dynasty unto himself. He has now won an unrivaled seven Super Bowl rings—one more than any individual NFL franchise—and has been named the big game's most valuable player a record five times. But none of what he has done matters as much to him as what is left to accomplish. When Brady said before the Super Bowl that his favorite championship is his next one, it reinforced an indomitable truth, one best articulated by Ben Shpigel in the *New York Times* the day after Super Bowl LV: When Tom Brady has something to prove, he is just about unbeatable.

SOURCE NOTES

The information contained in this book was derived from a great many sources—websites, news media, and a number of books. The list, as complete as I can manage, appears below. I apologize for any inadvertent omissions.

WEBSITES

Football-Reference.com offers extensive details, including the scores, box scores, and play-by-play accounts of every game, along with background details. It is a treasure trove of well-documented information, providing not only statistics but awards and milestones of players, past and present.

Other useful sites include:

New England Patriots home page:
www.patriots.com/team/players-roster/tom-brady/
Player profile of star quarterback Tom Brady

Tom Brady's Official Fan Page
www.facebook.com/TomBrady
Photos and videos posted by star player Tom Brady

NEWS MEDIA

Of the many online archives I explored, there are a few that provide an imposing volume of facts and observations, and therefore deserve special note:

Associated Press
Boston Globe
ESPN.com

New York Times

Sporting News

Sports Illustrated

TELEVISION AND VIDEO

"Tom Brady: The Winner—Patriots Quarterback Discusses His Career and Other Aspects of His Life," *60 Minutes* interview. Originally broadcast November 6, 2005, updated on December 20, 2007. www.cbsnews.com/news/tom-brady-the-winner.

The Brady 6, ESPN documentary, produced by NFL Films, 2011.

Tom vs. Time, six-part Facebook Watch reality docuseries, created by Gotham Chopra, released from January 25 to March 12, 2018.

BIBLIOGRAPHY

Boston Globe. *Greatness: The Rise of Tom Brady*. Chicago, IL: Triumph Books, 2005.

Brady, Tom. *The TB12 Method: How to Achieve a Lifetime of Sustained Peak Performance*. New York: Simon & Schuster, 2017.

Burt, Bill. "Raising a Champion: How Family, Competition and Love Helped Mold Tom Brady." *Eagle Tribune*, November 18, 2016.

Cafardo, Nick. *The Impossible Team: The Worst to First Patriots' Super Bowl Season*. Chicago, IL: Triumph Books, 2002.

Garber, Greg. "The Tom Brady Experience: Almost Perfect." ESPN.com, January 31, 2008.

Hohler, Bob. "Tom Brady's Humble Beginnings Here Had Hints of Greatness." *Boston Globe*, February 1, 2017.

Holley, Michael. *Belichick and Brady: Two Men, the Patriots, and How They Transformed the NFL*. New York: Hachette Books, 2016.

———. *Patriot Reign: Bill Belichick, the Coaches, and the Players Who Built a Champion*. New York: HarperCollins, 2009.

Jenkins, Sally. "Deflategate Got Tom Brady Mad, and the Rest of the NFL Is Paying the Price." *Washington Post*, November 6, 2015.

McGinn, Bob. " 'I Don't Like Him. Smart Guy. That's It.' What They Said about Tom Brady Before the 2000 Draft." *The Athletic*, September 25, 2019.

Myers, Gary. *Brady vs. Manning: The Untold Story of the Rivalry that Transformed the NFL*. New York: Crown Publishing Group, 2015.

O'Connor, Ian. *Belichick: The Making of the Greatest Football Coach of All Time*. New York: Houghton Mifflin Harcourt, 2018.

——. "Meet Tom Brady's First Believer." ESPN.com, January 16, 2015.

Pierce, Charles P. *Moving the Chains: Tom Brady and the Pursuit of Everything*. New York: Farrar, Straus and Giroux, 2006.

——. "The Ultimate Teammate." *Sports Illustrated*, December 12, 2005.

Sherman, Casey, and Dave Wedge. *12: The Inside Story of Tom Brady's Fight for Redemption*. Boston, MA: Little, Brown and Company, 2018.

Shoenfeld, Bruce. "Drew Bledsoe on Brady, Barolos, and Life after the NFL." ESPN.com, January 25, 2020.

Siegel, Alan. "The Last Bad Patriots Team." *The Ringer*, August 9, 2017.

Silver, Michael. "Cool Customer: Fresh Off a Storybook Season in Which He Quarterbacked the Patriots to a Super Bowl Victory at Age 24, Tom Brady Is Learning to Cope with the Blitz of Newfound Fame." *Sports Illustrated*, April 15, 2002.

Speros, Bill. "Before the GOAT: Tom Brady 'Could Have Been One of the Greatest Catchers Ever.' " *Bleacher Report*, June 2, 2017.

Stephens, Mitch. "Tom Brady Was No Goody Two Shoes at Serra High School." MaxPreps.com, January 31, 2015.

Thornton, Jerry. *Five Rings: The Super Bowl History of the New England Patriots (So Far)*. Lebanon, NH: University Press of New England, 2018.

Wolfe, Rich. *Tom Brady: There's No Expiration Date on Dreams*. Scottsdale, AZ: Lone Wolfe Press, 2002.

A NOTE OF APPRECIATION

MY FRIEND NIELS AABOE, SENIOR ACQUISITIONS EDITOR AT Globe Pequot/Lyons Press and a longtime advocate of my most recent books, helped to bring this project to fruition.

Melissa Hayes copy-edited the manuscript with insight and precision.

Amanda Wilson and Jason Rock created the graphic design and vivid layout of the pages you hold in your hands.

Mike Kopf proofread the manuscript chapter by chapter with care and discernment.

My son, Jack, kept tabs on my progress and offered some welcome and useful advice as I proceeded.

My wife, Carolyn, knew when I needed space to research, think, and write— and when I needed to be snapped back to reality.

ABOUT THE AUTHOR

David Fischer has written for the *New York Times* and *Sports Illustrated Kids* and has worked at *Sports Illustrated*, the *National Sports Daily*, and NBC Sports. He is the author of several sports titles, including *The New York Yankees of the 1950s: Mantle, Stengel, Berra and a Decade of Dominance*; *The Super Bowl: The First Fifty Years of America's Greatest Game*; *Aaron Judge: The Incredible Story of the New York Yankees' Home Run-Hitting Phenom*; *Derek Jeter #2: Thanks for the Memories*; *Big Papi: David Ortiz, Thanks for the Memories*; and *Miracle Moments in New York Yankees History*. Fischer is also the editor of *Facing Mariano Rivera*. He resides in New Jersey.